The Museum of Forward Planning

MUSEUM-SPLAINING

Tickets Unavailable
Museum of Forward Planning

Real stories from our imaginary museum

To the most contrary person I've ever known, with thanks.

We should all be more so

MOfP

Museum of forward planning

© 2023 Vidda Cartwright
ISBN: 9798376189436
All rights reserved.

Content

Part 1 - It's all about us

Welcome to MOfP 11

Unstructured organisational forms............................. 14

SWOT have you got?.. 25

Part 2 - It's all about you

Knowing your place... 30

Motivation and Wellbeing 42

Doing more, with less, more often 50

Operating a museum 62

Part 3 - It's all about them

The Visitor Journey 77

The Museum Exhibition 93

Collection responsibility.. 101

Marketing... 108

Part 4 - It's all about cash

Finding 'OUR' Audience 120

All about the money – Income Streaming 130

Selling out 135

Catering... 140

Capital project punishment. 143

Re-re-imaging the future 152

Illustrations

Figure 1 - The MOfP Messy Matrix Structure 15
Figure 2 Key attributes of the Executive team...................... 20
Figure 3 - The NPS explained 23
Figure 4 - Squeezing the pips from your middle managers .. 23
Figure 5 - The Circle of Career Fire... 31
Figure 6 - How to make decisions about visitor requirements 37
Figure 7 - Management compared with Leadership............. 38
Figure 8 - Incompetencies are key 39
Figure 9 - The balance - concentrating on 'being' in action .. 43
Figure 10 - The path to a happy workforce – balancing working locations.. 44
Figure 11 - But should life always be balanced? We concluded it's just not. 44
Figure 12 - A poster for our revolutionary 'Look after yourself' campaign.. 46
Figure 13 - Typical probing questions used in interviews throughout the sector.. 48
Figure 14 - Interview in progress 49
Figure 15 - Failure - always an option, whatever they tell you 51
Figure 16 - The point of maximum shame 53
Figure 17 – Gut instinct matters 54
Figure 18 - operational reality should be ignored 55
Figure 19 - Think outside your organisation 56
Figure 20 - Annoying your teams is key – operations is just a job, never a career 57
Figure 21 - The excitement gap 59
Figure 22 - The Triple 'T' Test.. 66

Figure 23 - Tricky, Tedious, Terrifying? Our constant refrain in operations 69
Figure 24 - Missing delegate syndrome 70
Figure 25 - The points of expectation move towards extrapolation... 73
Figure 26 - Smile Like You Mean it.. 75
Figure 27 - A simple visitor journey 78
Figure 28 - Ace of Base dispense their wisdom on signage .. 80
Figure 29 - The Base - Our signage strategy 81
Figure 30 and 31 - Some examples of effective signage 83
Figure 32 - Sometimes we can be too subtle....................... 84
Figure 33 - The signage imp 85
Figure 34 - The barrier banshee and cone orc..................... 86
Figure 35 - The barrier faerie 86
Figure 36 - The typo troll.. 87
Figure 37 - Queue like nobody is watching.......................... 89
Figure 38 - The infinity horn... 91
Figure 39 - The exhibition design card 96
Figure 40 - If only we could find some visitors to talk to 99
Figure 41 - A more realistic exhibition design approach 100
Figure 42 - The museum, and how we see it 103
Figure 43 - But is it worth looking at?................................. 104
Figure 44 - The 'Full Collins' 107
Figure 45 - Visit properly - our audience segregation work 121
Figure 46 - Loan Wolf 122
Figure 47 - Lost?122
Figure 48 - Emotional Backpacker....................................... 123
Figure 49 - Us 123
Figure 50 - Persecuted pedant 124
Figure 51 - Somnambulant scowler 124
Figure 52 - Personas... yawn 127

Figure 53 - MORON poster 131
Figure 54 - Pratrons 132
Figure 55 - The importance of leaving a legacy 134
Figure 56 - Sodding postcards 135
Figure 57 - Mugs 137
Figure 58 - Pay as you urn - an example of exciting innovation
.... 139
Figure 59 - Cake is no longer beyond the reach of mortals and museum staff 141
Figure 60 - Flantastic! Another great promotion 142
Figure 61 - Architectural outcomes 143
Figure 62 - One of many failed designs for future museums
.... 151
Figure 63 - The Truth 157

Forward

It's been a tough time in the Museum and Culture sector over the last few years.

It's been tough everywhere really, but let's be honest, we don't really care about anything else. Those of us who work and volunteer in the sector are all too aware that we are the thing that matters most to many, many people.

Back in 2020 when things seemed bleak in entirely different ways to the ways in which they seem bleak now, the Museum of Forward Planning was founded. It was intended to be a throwaway gag, a presentation for the always brilliant MuseumsShowoff (do look them up on twitter, and online!), but it didn't end there.

It turns out that nearly all our museums are run along the same principles and values as the imaginary museum of forward planning. At MOfP, we tried to articulate the ways in which all the work museum folk do is guided by our core principles.

We are Bold.

We are Brave.

And we are Batshit.

Museum professionals, and those who work in museums but remain entirely unprofessional, are guided by our desire to do great things. All the time. We are blind to the limitations of our finance, our mental health, our knowledge-base, and our experience.

Above all we are blind to our visitors and to that moment where our well-laid plans come into contact with our well-intentioned visitors, a process which is refereed by our less than well-paid teams.

At times MOfP has been a little scathing. At times we have delivered our verdict on the sector with extreme side-eye, and with a huge amount of hypocrisy. These are often universal ways of working, and they are not just unique to Museums. Though of course we **know** that no other sector in the world is as unique as we are.

In the course of our commentary via sociable media (led by me and the members of the Catering (Pork Scratchings) Sub-Committee) it has become apparent that a guide on how not to run a museum is at least as vital as any self-help book.

So here is ours. Well, volume one anyway.

#MembersOnly

(And SHHH, but we do LOVE museums and culture really)

MOfP
Museum of forward planning

Geoff.

Part 1

It's all about us

Chapter 1

Welcome to MOfP
Re-re-imagining the museum

You've probably never visited us. We probably don't exist. But we think we do.

We think we exist in all museums and galleries. We think we exist in the meeting rooms, on the zoom calls, in the unread minutes and the papers on practice. We think we're absurd. And we think you are too.

The Museum of Forward Planning was established at the height of the pandemic, when the world was reeling, when we didn't know what would come next, and when, in those early days as the world disintegrated the talk of rebuilding was only of 'building back better'.

We haven't built back better of course. We've built back the same. We're just human.

MOfP shines a light on the absurdity of the way we often work. But at the heart we have a clarity of mission and vision that we're proud of.

RE-RE-IMAGINED

A vision you can't see.

'To retain and explain the efforts of operations teams to deliver visitor experience in an ever-changing world, whilst remaining sane'

'Making sure your knowledge is actively forgotten, not passively ignored'

We aim.

- To preserve and share the numerous excel workbooks of reworked operational priorities.

- To further understanding of the volume of salt-water tears shed by operational teams.

- To build upon our core values which define museum operations as anything other teams define as TRICKY, TEDIOUS or TERRIFYING

- *To pass off our quiet terror as deep confidence at all times.*

For a future you can't believe in

We will create a bright future.

MOfP – the museum where operational planning comes to die.

A space for fallen stanchions. Room to place buckets that catch the tears of Estate teams. Insufficient toilets and lifts that are INTENDED to fail!

In one place, we will gather the failures, the vanity projects and the fallen egos of our sector. Follow us – if you can work out the orientation.

Of course. This could not possibly exist. No museum would work like this. Would it?

Chapter 2

Unstructured organisational forms

This chapter will explore the matrix structure so beloved of our deeply siloed museums, where creative tension is used as an excuse to deliver stress for all. We will examine the key elements of museum leadership and the best methods of communication to apply for each of these teams.

'We're too big for that to work here'.

'Museums are just very complicated spaces.

'We operate a matrix management structure'.

How often have you heard these statements as you've raised issues about the siloed nature of your place of work? Well, don't worry, that's the same everywhere. And the reason for that? Museum leadership usually aren't museum managers. And museum managers, generally haven't had a lot of management training.

Ah, an easy claim to make.

Agreed, and that's because it's absolutely true.

Just because you can spot a knock out artwork, set up an outstanding exhibition, or deliver a lecture on the one thing you are the world expert on. That doesn't mean for one minute that you're actually any good at running an organisation.

In this chapter we'll be looking at the most common organisational structure within museums. This hasn't been easy. In most cases the structure of the museums and galleries we work in changes so often it's hard to capture. In the remainder, the organisational structure charts have not been updated since the late 1980's and are largely held in archive.

Let's begin by looking at the 'Messy Matrix Structure' as employed here at MOfP.

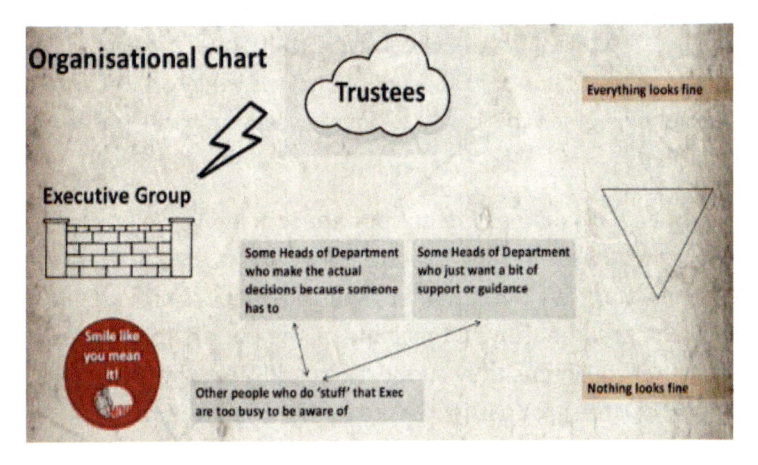

Figure 1 - The MOfP Messy Matrix Structure

The Messy Matrix Structure

Many organisations claim to operate a matrix structure. This is a neat way of explaining that there aren't any clear lines of accountability and responsibility and that actually everything just floats between departments with nobody having the final say.

Here at MOfP we're proud to work to a clear structure. We know exactly the game we're playing and how it works.

Organisations in the museum and heritage sector are, of course, all about the visitor. That's so much of a given that there is absolutely no need to mention them anywhere here.

Let's take a look at how the key groups interact.

Trustees

It's very clear that the Trustees are here to support and nurture the talent on the Executive Group. Imagine Gods in those cartoons you saw as a child, or even the more recent Marvel Universe. This is what Trustees are, only less based in reality.

Our board of Trustees are appointed from a diverse pool of people who are already Trustees everywhere else. This ensures that they don't need to read the papers provided (as they can assume they're the same as the papers provided at the other museums they support). In addition, the diversity of our Trustee group is increased by the intervention of government and big businesses.

Essentially the role of a Trustee is to email or call asking for complimentary tickets for friends and family, and to pick a particular area of expertise where they can provide insight that was otherwise lacking. This will include information about running Hedge Funds, International Law, and there must be at least one Trustee who is elected to the Board entirely to ask about some random item in the shop that they think the museum should stock more of. This item will be postcards.

Communicating with Trustees

The exact approach here will largely depend on whether the Executive Team of your organisation are busy worrying about whether the Trustees are about to uncover their deep-seated fear and incompetence, or whether the Trustee Board are worried that the Executive Team of your organisation are about to uncover their deep-seated fear and incompetence.

Communication approaches often depend on the Chair. But options range from:

1. **The thunderbolt** – this style of communication involves sudden and unexpected lightning bolts being thrown from the Trustees. These are often (but not exclusively) aimed at specific Directors who they either like or dislike intensely. The thunderbolt may strike at all levels of the organisation. Burning any levels of management or leadership between the Trustee and the desired target.
2. **The scattergun** – this approach will include frequent and florid emails. Usually sent in a format that suggests the Trustees are unaware that they actually employ an Executive Team to run the organisation and it is not, in fact, their role to decide what approach the organisation takes to interpretation, collection care, income generation and postcard ranges.
3. **The presence** – this approach is preferred by those members of the Trustee Board who most enjoy saying 'don't you know who I am?'. Key considerations here are

that most front of house staff either don't know who the person is, or if they do are *painfully* aware, consider it a travesty that such an individual is involved in the museum and will therefore pretend they do not know who the individual is. This communication form is therefore ignored.

The Executive Team

You'll meet the Executive Team, from time to time they'll be making decisions based on many hours of your hard work and careful consideration. In all Museums the team will largely consist of well-regarded colleagues in the industry. They'll be brilliant people in their field. Their field will be largely curatorial and will tend to have very little crossover with their day-to-day role of leading and directing a large organisation that really needs a strong leadership team that puts people and development at the heart of all the organisation does.

There are some key considerations which are vital to ensuring anything that happens on the floor of your museum is understood, even on the vaguest level, by those people on the Executive team who make all the key decisions.

Communicating with the Executive Team

In the messy matrix structure preferred by MOfP there are a number of important elements to consider in all presentations to the Executive team.

1. **Brevity** - Members of the executive are highly talented, deep thinkers. They are capable of working across

organisations and of producing lengthy keynote speeches for conferences and detailed, well-argued papers for academic consideration. As a result they have no time to consider how your museum runs. All communication needs to be in the form of a 'paper'. This must consist of no more than one page of A4 and have a maximum of three bullet points for consideration.
2. **Witless** - All papers presented to the Executive team require you to present clear options for them to choose between. If you have worked with young children or animals consider options such as 'do you want beans or cheese on toast?'. Of the two options presented the Executive team will always choose option three. Option three needs to be something you have fully considered previously and discounted as unworkable. You need to be prepared to explain this, and then implement option three in any case.
3. **Powerless** - Executive teams are very keen on empowerment. Empowerment means that you, as a lowly member of the staff, and paid several times less than them, will be expected to come up with the solutions the organisation requires, to implement them, and then to take feedback when they don't work because they have received insufficient support from the Executive team. Remember, just because your Executive team signs something off, it does not mean they understood it.

Museum Of Forward Planning

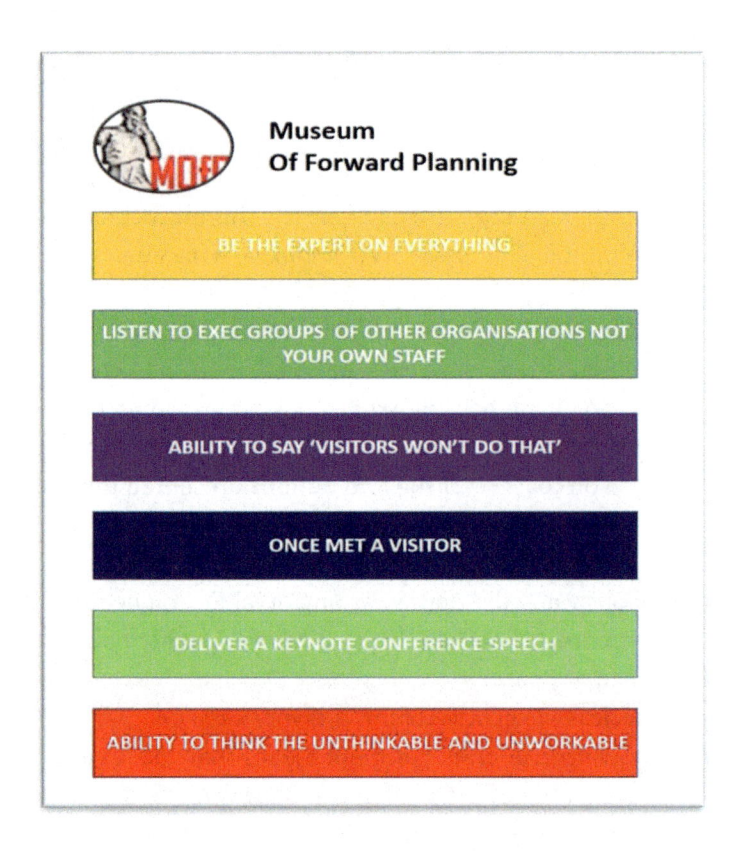

- BE THE EXPERT ON EVERYTHING
- LISTEN TO EXEC GROUPS OF OTHER ORGANISATIONS NOT YOUR OWN STAFF
- ABILITY TO SAY 'VISITORS WON'T DO THAT'
- ONCE MET A VISITOR
- DELIVER A KEYNOTE CONFERENCE SPEECH
- ABILITY TO THINK THE UNTHINKABLE AND UNWORKABLE

Figure 2 Key attributes of the Executive team

Senior Leadership Team

There's always a senior leadership team. It's very important that your museum keeps this separate from the executive team. This enables the Executive team to dream the big dreams, while the Senior Leadership team spend their lives trying to deal with the crunch point where the unrealistic aspirations of the Board of Trustees and the Executive team have to come into contact with the real world and will, inevitably, dissolve.

The Senior Leadership team will vary greatly in terms of make-up, size and the portfolios they operate. The key element of creating such a team is to understand that they will complete all the elements of running the museum that are too difficult for anyone above or below them to want to get mixed up in.

The Senior Leadership team will comprise a core of people who actually take all the decisions in the organisation, and a cluster who support them, until it is proved that the wrong decisions have been taken.

Communicating with the Senior Leadership Team

This team of people will always be the most stressed and at the centre of the organisation. There are some key things to consider in all communication. For the purpose of this team, we need to consider communication both 'up' and 'down' the chain (as illustrated in figure 2)

The main channels to communicate with this key team will be.

1. **Emails**. Emails should be sent at all hours, all days of the week. Always. It is essential though to note that sometimes even this team may need a rest. On days off and holidays it is therefore appropriate to preface any communication with 'I know you're away/off but…'

2. **Teams / Slack / Zoom**. If the last two years have taught us anything it is that emails are not sufficiently life-sapping, and we can now ensure that our senior teams are bombarded through numerous channels at all times of the day and night. Ideally your organisation will agree on a preferred channel, and then continue to use What's App.
3. **Phone calls.** Nobody uses the phone now, apart from this team. They'll be on call pretty much for their entire lives. It's vital to ensure they are equipped with a smartphone that gives a slightly sub-optimal performance in order to generate the additional stress needed to get these colleagues the adrenaline kick they need to deal with any major incident.
4. **Face to face meetings** so old-school, we thought they'd gone with the advent of zoom and teams, but no! Now you can have zoom, teams AND meet as well to discuss the online meetings onsite. Like virtual meetings, but you can't pretend the Wi-fi went down so you have to pay attention.

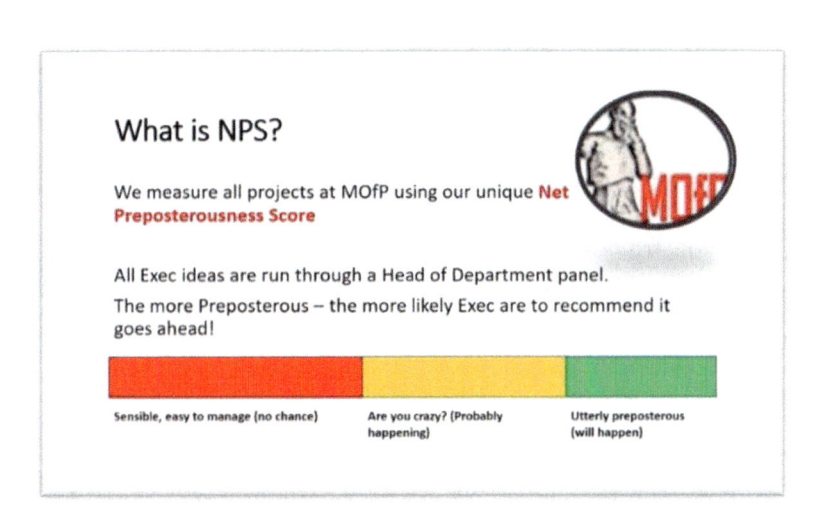

Figure 3 - The NPS explained

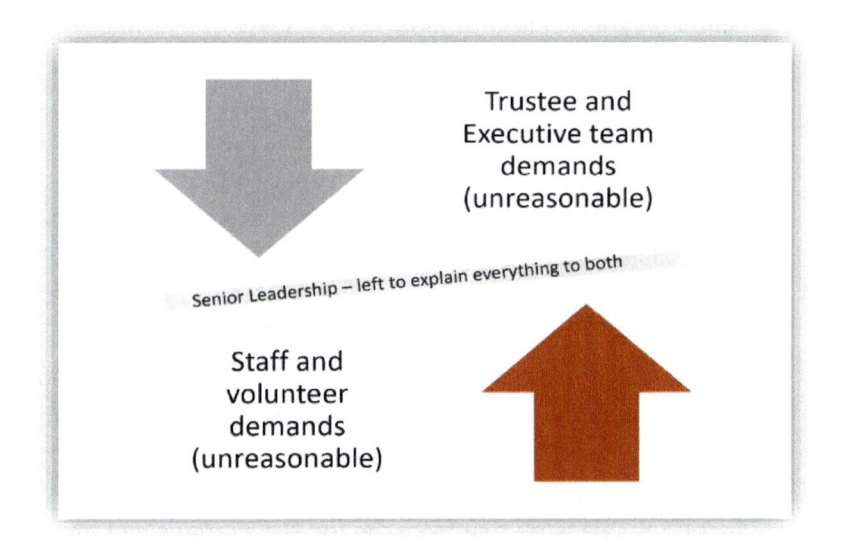

Figure 4 - Squeezing the pips from your middle managers

Other people who do stuff the Exec are unaware of

Clearly the areas covered above are by far the smallest proportion of any museum or gallery. But, we all know, they're essentially the only ones that count.

If you are one of the other people-who-do-stuff it's vital to be aware that the important people care deeply about what you do, how you feel and your own personal career development. They don't care enough to do anything about this though because they're very busy.

It is incredibly hard for people-who-do-stuff to gain entry into the higher echelons of the organisation. Progress is usually best achieved by taking everything you have learned and tried to communicate upwards to another organisation. For a limited period of time when you take a new role, you'll notice that everything you say is seen as sensible, achievable and will be implemented. Sadly, over time, you will begin to become invisible again. Enjoy the visibility while you can, but do take care not to become accidentally empowered as once you are in the Senior Leadership team there is often no way to escape. Other than teaching.

Conclusion

There are other organisational structures, but museums and cultural organisations prefer the creative tension (or stress) that we've already described. The key element to maintaining progress towards delivery of your cause is to continue to ensure that from the top – everything looks rosy.

Chapter 3

SWOT have you got?

Nobody likes a swot – or so we are told by idiots.

Yet, everyone does SWOT analysis on their organisation and the process in itself is always worth your time and effort.

Of course, museums are often a hotbed of 'Silo-ism' so it is likely that any SWOT analysis will be completed by each team in complete and glorious isolation.

To consider the different approaches to museums we have shared below a few of the differing SWOT analyses completed by MOfP's diverse teams.

It should be noted that shortly after this Retail/Commercial and Curatorial/ Collections Care were merged. With devastating results.

Curatorial SWOT

Strengths	Weaknesses
The amazing Curatorial team All the amazing items in our collections That mahogany desk set that is the 13th best of the type in France. The fact other curators admire us. Our great works of research. The opportunity to feature on BBC4 and Radio 4	Visitors Volunteers Staff who want to talk to visitors. Staff who want to talk to curators. Volunteers who want to talk to curators. Volunteers who want to talk to staff. Budgets (WTF?!)

Opportunities	Threats
MORE words about MORE things	Anything 'Commercial'
A bigger collection, acquired more quickly.	Anything that attracts 'the wrong' visitors.
More information and education of visitors	Anything that generates income.
Acquiring the 14th best mahogany desk set from France.	Any suggestion the collection is dull or too big.
A future exhibition on a pet topic that will be expensive and only attract 'the right' visitors.	Any suggestion there are TOO MANY WORDS
A Channel 5 fly-on-the-wall documentary	Signage to help visitors around the site.
Podcasts	Another curator writing the book before me.
	Another curator on BBC4 or Radio 4

Collections Care SWOT

Strengths	Weaknesses
The museum is dark.	People want lights.
The museum is cold but dry.	People want warmth.
Very few people come to the museum.	People want to eat and drink.
	People want to visit.
The collection is safely stored.	People make dust.
No visitors at night	People touch things they shouldn't.
No visitors when we are closed.	People smell things they shouldn't.
Curators have not found the cataloguing database	People lick things they shouldn't
Opportunities	**Threats**
We could close more.	Staff
We could drive visitors' numbers lower.	Visitors
	Light
We could turn down the light.	Heat
We could turn down the heat.	Cold
We could put all the collection away safely forever.	Dryness
	Damp
	Bugs and pest (see visitors)
	Dust
	Curators

Executive Group SWOT

Strengths	Weaknesses
The Museum has a brilliant Board. The Museum has brilliant Trustees The Museum hosts brilliant events Everyone loves working at the museum. There is no reason to doubt our mission The museum has an amazing, relevant, and exciting cause. The Museum is all that matters. There is nothing that cannot be solved in a half-page executive summary and 3 bullet points.	Sometimes some of those staff seem a bit grumpy. We have to pay some people. We once went in on a Saturday and there were 'people'. We probably shouldn't have taken money from the sale of blood diamonds. The roof does leak a bit.
Opportunities	**Threats**
We could do more, with less, more often, with greater enthusiasm, lower expenditure, and greater efficiency. Postcards. There's an exhibition we've always wanted to do that nobody is interested in, but it will be an absolute blockbuster if we charge £50 a ticket and Grenville lends us that contested object from the BM at a huge cost and with very tricky loan agreements.	Have you seen the Government? Some of those visitors sound intense. Staff. Sometimes the wine is a little off at opening events and our friends are less keen.

Front of House SWOT

Strengths	Weaknesses
The Front of House teams (Obviously) That's it really. It's not that we have a chip on our shoulders, but we don't think anyone else is necessary. We love the collection, and the museum, and some visitors.	All the other teams. Members. Especially Members. The Executive teams Management Pay Terms and Conditions We have to have too many visitors to make the finances stack up. We don't like too many visitors.

Opportunities	Threats
Fire the Board	The Government
Fire the Managers	The Board
Ban the Members	The Managers
Reduce the number of visitors.	The Members
Open fewer hours	Anything that in any way affects the purity that we perceive we deliver to our visitors (whether they want it or not)
Decent coffee in the canteen	
A canteen	
Postcards	

Conclusion

We have only covered a small number of our teams, but you get the general gist.

Retail and Catering colleagues merely scrawled the word 'SELL' in red biro across the entire exercise, and so had to be excluded from the strategic plan as they were proving to be too commercial. Instead MOfP was pleased to be able to set up a separate company where colleagues can be employed on inferior pay and conditions in order to deliver much needed revenue for the organisation, whilst those who work in the charitable area can ensure they remain unsullied.

As can be seen from this simple exercise, the teams have far more in common than they would be prepared to share. And our much derided, yet powerfully defended silo structure ensures the carefully balance 'creative tension' of the museum remains as highly strung as is possible for the maximum period of time.

Part 2

It's all about you

Chapter 4

Knowing your place

In this chapter we will be exploring how a career in museums, heritage and culture can be most accurately described, how best to understand your place in the sector, and sharing a few tips on the best way to achieve a salary that just about covers the rent.

The performative act of a museum career

'Find a job you love, and you'll never work a day in your life'.

'Find a job you love, and you'll lose all sense of work/life separation and spiral towards stress and negativity whilst the institution you love ignores all the signs'.

Both of these are familiar quotes to anyone who has worked for more than a season in the Museums sector.

At MOfP we have really taken the time to consider the most popular career life-cycle because we recognise that transparency is important, and that once an employee is of no more use to us it is essential we have considered the most humane way to dispose of the empty husk.

Our Career Cycle

There are a number of stages to anyone's career in the culture sector.

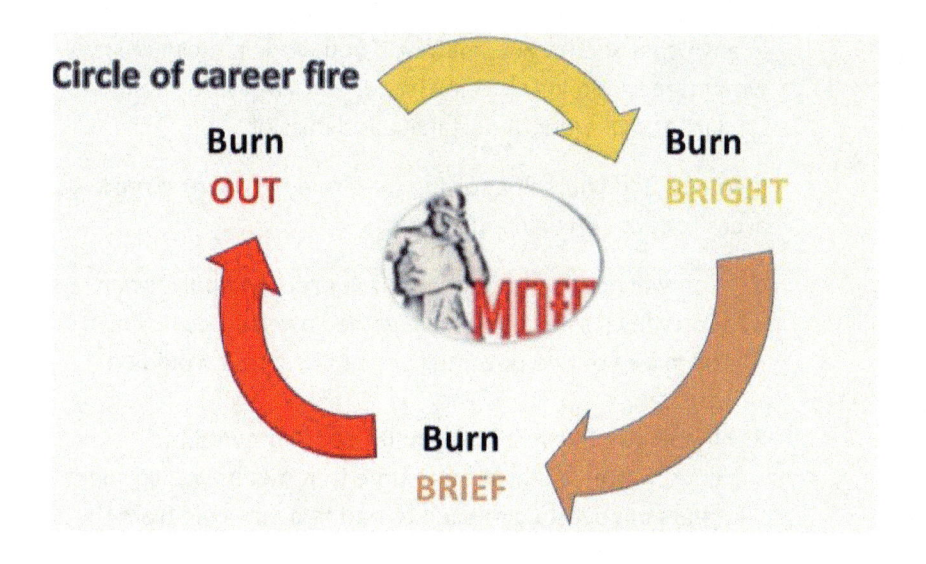

Figure 5 - The Circle of Career Fire

Getting the job

Initially your main consideration is, of course, getting that dream role in the sector. Hopefully this chapter can help you to think about how that might work.

Undoubtedly, it's going to be tough. There are always many hundreds of thousands of people competing for each role. Museums are renowned for our ability to ensure the process remains as opaque as possible.

Ideally of course you'll love museums so much that you won't need any payment at all and so can volunteer for one of our volunteer opportunities that read suspiciously like a paid job in any other sector. Fortunately, if you work in museums, you won't need food, drink or shelter. It will simply be enough to be part of our wider undertaking and mission.

If you do find yourself applying for a role there are some key areas to focus on any application.

1. You will need at least one PhD in order to apply for an entry level role. If you have gained a very specific PhD from one of two potential universities, that would be great.
2. If you don't have a PhD you'll need 'comparable experience'. It's best to assume that means you've spent years in poverty, are used to eating beans cold from the can and have no aspiration to move beyond an entry level role.
3. You will be expected to tell us that the only place you have ever wanted to work, ever, is our museum and that you'll be fine achieving all the thirty-five different points on the job description and that you speak several languages fluently.
4. In the near future most National Museums and arms-length government bodies will, of course, expect you to have at least a first degree in Maths.

So, you've made it through the selection process and you've finally been offered a role in the dream museum. Once you've sorted out relocating to a different area of the country at your own expense, it's time to consider how best to get the most out of your career. Here we can help, with our bespoke three-point plan

Burn Bright

The first stage of any museum and heritage career is 'burn bright'. During this period, you will genuinely experience the wonder of working in a creative, exciting, dynamic and ever-changing sector. In museums, you'll find there is no such word as 'can't', or indeed 'shouldn't'. While many well-funded and commercially viable organisations, with far larger payrolls and greater depth of knowledge will turn away from running activities and events outside their core mission statement and objectives – that's not going to be the case here!

Let's consider just how exciting this is.

Burning Bright – Case Study

Mencer and Sparks are an established retailer, they've been selling clothes and food for over a hundred years. They are suddenly presented with the opportunity to take on work in a range of new areas. With less than 4 weeks' notice they've been asked to deliver the following:

1. A multi-day festival including key headline acts, and an attendance of several times their weekly number of customers in just two days.

It is going to involve setting up and delivering in a whole range of areas; catering, toilets and infrastructure, an entirely new ticketing approach, parking, and logistics plans.

Risk assessments, additional staffing, management time and working with a creative team who have yet to develop the content, marketing or offer.

> Imagine you work at Mencer and Sparks – what would your approach be?
>
> **Outcome**
>
> We all know how this will turn out. Mencer and Sparks, with their multi-million pound budgets for staffing, marketing and their years of logistics experience, with their thousands of staff, will not touch this with a barge poll. This isn't their business.
>
> That's why you should be delighted to work in the culture sector. In the culture sector none of the above would be an issue. Where angels fear to tread, and without any consideration of the risks, costs or stress entailed, you can guarantee your Executive team are going to sign you up for this and it will be an 'incredible opportunity' for you and your team.

This is what 'Burn Bright' is all about.

You'll find yourself leading on areas of work you never even considered would be yours, at the same time as delivering the 'day job'. Day jobs, in museums, it should be noted do not take any time to deliver.

No other career gives you so much opportunity, so fast and so frequently.

Burn Brief

Most people in museums experience that brief period, that high, when they have achieved everything that was asked of them. This is your moment. The grand opening of that exhibition you worked on for two years, the delivery of the festival or weekend of activities that the funding was all targeted for, or the shift in demographics at your site because you delivered a programme that people actually wanted to take part in!

Savour this.

For both the hours you have time to consider it.

What museums really like to do is to move on immediately to the next thing. Yes, you might still be delivering the exhibition for another 12 months as it opens every day, but that takes no effort or thought. Already, your senior team have moved on to the next exhibition and so must you.

It is a vital part of every cultural organisation that you constantly re-invent everything. You MUST re-re-reimagine a more immersive experience, and try not to sink beneath the waves of creativity. Of course, the visitors are only just getting used to the latest iteration of your space, of course the staff have only just completed their training to bring the museum to life, but the push for funding requires an immediate move to something new. Better prepare the candle and set fire to both ends, as you run the current proposition while preparing the next.

Burn Out

Ah.

Maybe skip this bit if you are relatively new to your role.

Essentially you are now on the treadmill. Visitor feedback will be collated, staff feedback may be collated, even staff feedback about visitors feedback may be collated (if you work for an enlightened and forward thinking museum). As the information is collected it will be filed.

The information will illustrate everything you've been saying about the latest projects.

- They've engaged the target audience.
- The team have loved delivering them.
- The visitor flow didn't work as everyone expected but we tweaked it and got it right in the end.
- The toilets and lifts weren't sufficient.
- You and your team were right about the capacity
- The changes you made to access and interpretation really worked.
- The parallel schools programme was a huge success.

All of the above will be ignored. Instead, after it has been filed, the new project will make every single mistake the old project made despite your suggestions, then your protest, and finally, you will lose the will.

Sorry about that.

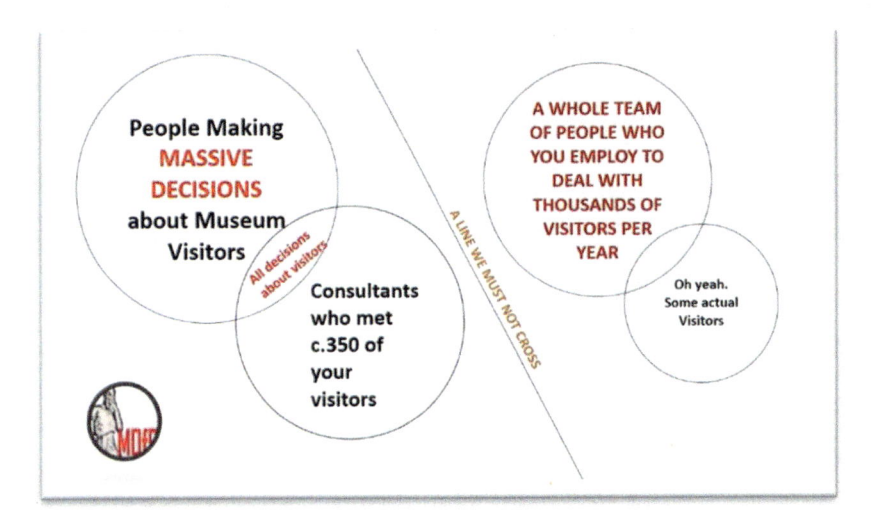

Figure 6 - How to make decisions about visitor requirements

Personal Development

Like many in the museum sector MOfP has proudly delivered a very self-led development programme. If you want to develop yourself, by all means, crack on.

Management Roles

It's key that anyone fulfilling a management role in a museum and culture sector environment should largely be there because they have a huge amount of curatorial and content knowledge. You can easily pick up the bit about people management at some point in the future.

Stuff (in the form of collections, historic buildings and the fabric of history) is, as we all know, far more important than staff. What do people offer other than additional workload and ongoing pain?

If you find yourself unlucky enough to be placed in a management role there are a number of things you need to carefully consider. The first of these is that you will need to decide whether to exude either 'Management' or 'Leadership'. Most management self-help books are clear it is impossible to be both, so you must choose widely.

To be honest, at MOfP, we prize 'Leadership' above 'Management'. Primarily this is because there is a vagueness attached to the idea of leadership that is both harder to performance manage against, and sounds inherently more creative.

Nobody wants to be a 'thought manager' when you can be a 'thought leader'.

Management vs Leadership in Museums

Management	Leadership
• Requires 20/20 vision	• 'Inspires' vague future visions
• Detail's the rage	• Stick to one page
• Vital due diligence	• Ignorance of our legal defence
• There for your team	• Persons unseen
• There when you call	• Have just dropped the ball

Figure 7 - Management compared with Leadership

Competence is key.

Nobody is quite sure how or why, but competence is most certainly key. It is the role of management in the museum to insist upon competence whilst also maintaining an air of harassed incompetence at all times.

Managers are widely viewed as incompetent because their position involves attempting to deliver the dreams of an Executive team which are so far from reality it is clearly unachievable. At the same time managers must show complete loyalty to the vision that is being projected by both the Executive team and the Trustees (especially on the subject of postcards).

Management Incompetencies

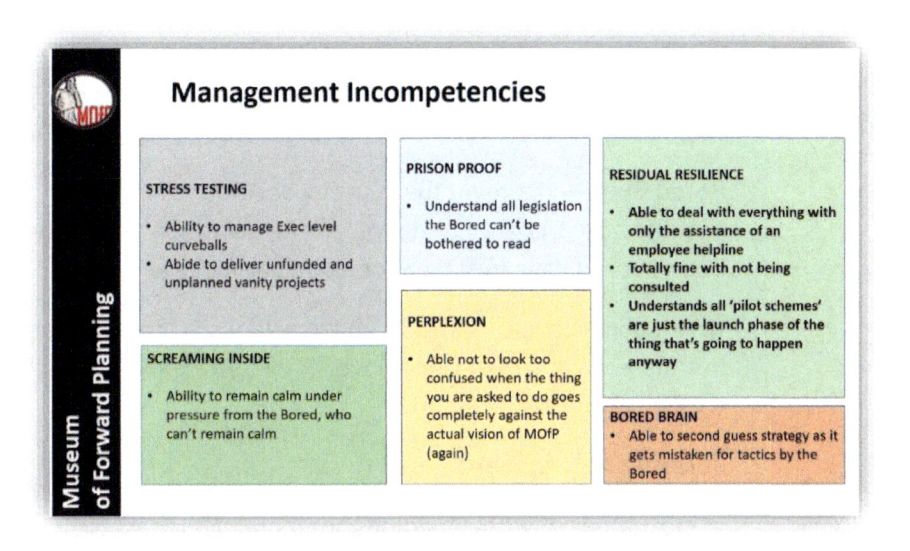

STRESS TESTING
- Ability to manage Exec level curveballs
- Abide to deliver unfunded and unplanned vanity projects

SCREAMING INSIDE
- Ability to remain calm under pressure from the Bored, who can't remain calm

PRISON PROOF
- Understand all legislation the Bored can't be bothered to read

PERPLEXION
- Able not to look too confused when the thing you are asked to do goes completely against the actual vision of MOfP (again)

RESIDUAL RESILIENCE
- Able to deal with everything with only the assistance of an employee helpline
- Totally fine with not being consulted
- Understands all 'pilot schemes' are just the launch phase of the thing that's going to happen anyway

BORED BRAIN
- Able to second guess strategy as it gets mistaken for tactics by the Bored

Museum of Forward Planning

Figure 8 - Incompetencies are key

Turning Competencies inside out

Since we have effectively explained competencies are an irrelevant busted flush, it makes sense to 'dial down' our emphasis on the approach and to manage expectations.

The focus areas at MOfP are in the areas outlined in figure 8.

Stress Testing – is all about being able to deliver vanity projects which do not appear in any plan.

Prison Proof – is the ability to review and translate legal requirements, thus protecting the Board/Bored.

Screaming Inside – reflects the need to maintain a poker face at all times as random demands rise.

Perplexion – is a focus on demonstrating performance skills, so that when the Board requests you to deliver something that runs contrary to all vision and plans, you can style it out.

Bored Brain – whatever the strategy documents and priorities, be prepared to deliver a range of tactics which the Board/Bored have mistaken for an actual strategy.

Residual resilience – basically covers every other area of life in a museum at a managerial level. Previously known as 'YOYO' – You're on your own.

Personal development

In most areas of work, ongoing career and personal development is a key consideration in all roles and all levels of an organisation.

Thankfully at MOfP we do not need to consider any of this. It is enough just to work for us and be part of our industry.

In order to deliver the levels of resilience the sector will require in the future resilience will be vital.

Self-Directed

'Self-direction is the only direction, any other direction is mis-direction.'

This quote from our outgoing Head of HR, sums up the approach we must all take to developing our careers. In line with the residual resilience (YOYO – You're on your own) approach. MOfP, like many modern museum and cultural organisations, has taken the approach that it is better for people to strive and fail on their own, than for them to be strive and fail at the expense of the museum.

There's nothing more to be said on personal development. It's a very personal thing and has no place in a wider discussion of the lack of management skill and support in the cultural sector.

Chapter 5

Motivation and Wellbeing
#LookAfterYourself

For many years we knew that wellbeing at work was important. At MOFP we often talk about work-life balance. This is a lot easier than actually doing anything about it.

As a rule of thumb, the more a workplace discusses 'work-life balance' the less they care. 'saying is displaying' as our outgoing HR Director once said, as they took early retirement, sacked off the final salary pension scheme on the way out, and became a 'lifestyle coach'.

Our unique #LookAfterYourself campaign has, in part, been shaped by the fires of the pandemic.

This enabled us to take a step back and consider fully how we could 'build back better'. Like much of the sector we decided we couldn't necessarily manage that, but we knew how to bulldoze better – so that's what we did. And then we added yoga.

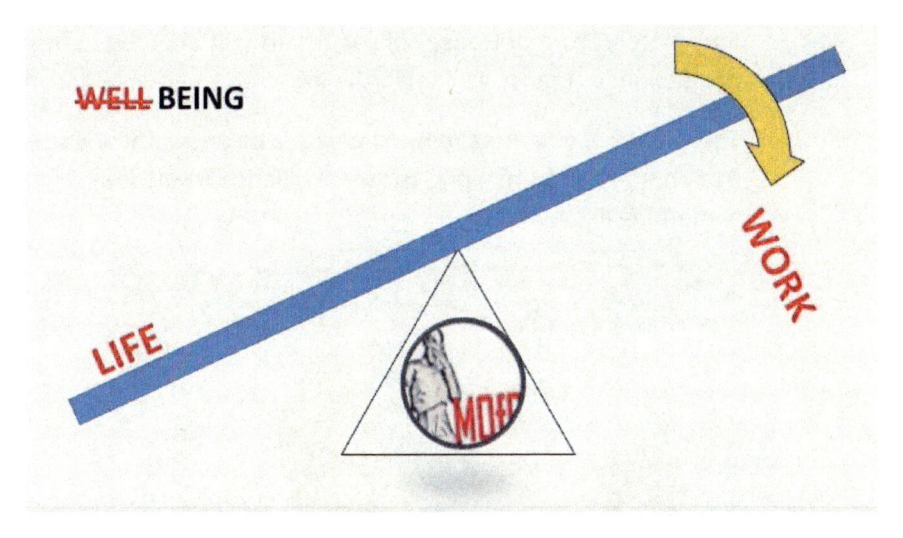

Figure 9 - The balance - concentrating on 'being' in action

If you feel work is taking over your life, one simple solution is to remove the barriers and choose life.

To do this museums are fond of taking the opportunity to restructure or provide people with incredibly flexible roles (or as we call them, fixed term contracts).

It's all in the blend.

As we saw during Covid, it's very possible for large numbers of the museum workforce to do their roles from home. This means they have even less of a chance of accidentally coming into contact with visitors. This is known as a 'win-win', because really, most museum professionals have very little interest in museum visitors. They're a little like oil and water.

Fortunately Front of House colleagues are not deemed to be professionals as anyone can do the job.

This means, if you are aiming to create a balance of working from home and from work, the ideal balance would look something like figure 9.

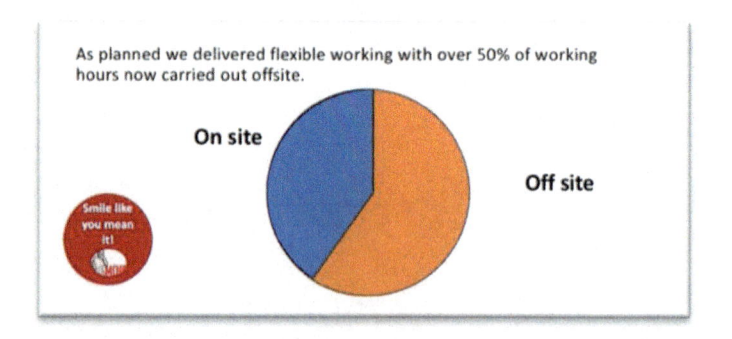

Figure 10 - The path to a happy workforce – balancing working locations

It's important to note that the balance is achieved equitably. Figure 11 below highlights that this is easily achieved with a sensible division across teams.

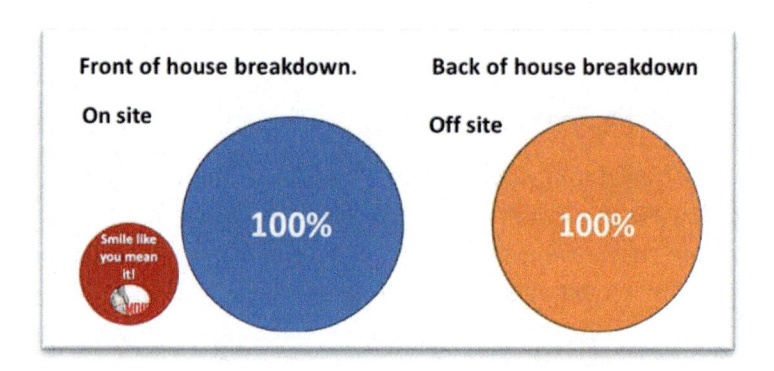

Figure 11 - But should life always be balanced? We concluded it's just not.

The front of house teams like being onsite anyway, it's not as if they can't afford the costs of travel given their massive salaries.

Staff Survey

If, like us, the happiness of your staff is important, you'll need to have a way to measure it.

The best method is to force all your teams to complete a questionnaire during their unpaid breaks. It is ideal to have these completed just after the failed pay negotiations and during the busiest months of the year.

It's no good just asking staff to complete the survey. For maximum results a number of elements are important.

1. Management must be held to account. If the happiness score for a team is low, the obvious next step is to sack the middle manager who is only doing what they were instructed by their senior managers, and does not have the budget or agency to affect change.
2. It will be necessary to produce an extensive action plan to resolve key issues. This needs unrealistic timescales and no associated budget. You should aim to ensure the priorities to achieve happy staff, are in direct conflict with the requirements of keeping your museum or gallery afloat financially.
3. A section of the feedback should allow individuals to make unacceptable comments about Directors, line managers and anyone they don't like. This will be anonymous so the maximum invective can be imparted. There will be no right of reply.

4. DO NOT complete a survey of how managers feel. You don't want to know, and you don't appear to care.

Well-being programme

A well-being programme MUST include yoga. You don't need anyone to attend more than once, you don't need anyone to enjoy it and you won't have much outlay as a friend of a friend of one of the Directors will have recently set up as a yoga teacher and will happily run the first few sessions for free. That's plenty to get the posters up in the staff areas.

At MOFP we've simplified our well-being campaign, in order to align it with our processes that help us do more, with less, more often, with less budget and with greater enthusiasm.

We simply focus ourselves and our teams on being.

Figure 12 - A poster for our revolutionary 'Look after yourself' campaign

A good programme will also include some of the following elements.

An extensive online webinar offers.

This should be available to only back of house staff, and should largely cover the kind of stress you only experience as a front of house colleague.

Social events

These should not be fun. They should be held at times that are inconvenient for front of house staff or aim for a weekend because 'everyone will be off' apart from the actual majority of your workforce.

Say supportive things.

There are a range of useful phrases that can be employed to give the impression you care. This should include; 'you should not be afraid to say no' (unless you value your job and resent being labelled as negative), 'we really want you to take time out' (send reminder emails to all colleagues out of hours). Whilst you MUST say these things it is essential not to commit any of it in writing. We won't be covering employment law, for obvious reasons.

Building Resilience

How often have we heard the phrase 'belt up sunshine, it could be worse'? Not anywhere frequently enough if you were to ask our outgoing Director Of Happiness here at MOfP.

While it's lovely to offer people a shoulder to cry on, supportive yoga, and well-being seminars that mean they have to work late at home to make up for the 'lost time' at work. Sometimes we need more, and sometimes that's also important for future career development too.

Anyone who has applied for the next role in a museum hierarchy (museums aren't hierarchical but a good hierarchy is important and very much established in most), will be aware that one of the key questions you will need to be able to answer will be about your resilience.

How much shit can you put up with and continue to smile.

Tell me about a time you.	This demonstrates...
Had convince your boss they were an idiot without letting on you knew they were an idiot	**Resilience**
Had to deal with a difficult situation without any support from Senior Managers	
Were left crying because of the sheer terror of the workload and demands of Trustees	

Figure 13 - Typical probing questions used in interviews throughout the sector

While everyone at MOfP is committed to saying supportive words out loud. We know, and so should anyone in the sector, that this largely performative.

Figure 14 - Interview in progress

Chapter 6

Doing more, with less, more often
Strategy matters

At this stage we've covered many of the basics of career and team management within museums and cultural attractions. However, it's time to turn our attention the most vital ingredient in any successful organisation in the Arts sector.

Before we reach the operational and planning stages of running a museum, we need to consider how we can entrap the teams responsible for delivering our ideas, into actually believing it is achievable.

Many management books will raise the valid point that performance reviews, appraisals and development plans are key to a happy workforce. There is some validity in this, but not in the case of the culture sector. These are the same books that suggest you set SMART objectives which can be easily measured and should be limited in number so that colleagues can focus on delivery and won't be overwhelmed.

At MOfP we know that culture IS overwhelming for all kinds of reasons. If it was easy to work in a museum we wouldn't need really clever people like curators and directors, we could leave it to idiots like you. We can't. It would be a disaster.

As our director always says – 'there is an 'I' in failure' and that's you.

There is an 'I' in failure. And 'U,R' too

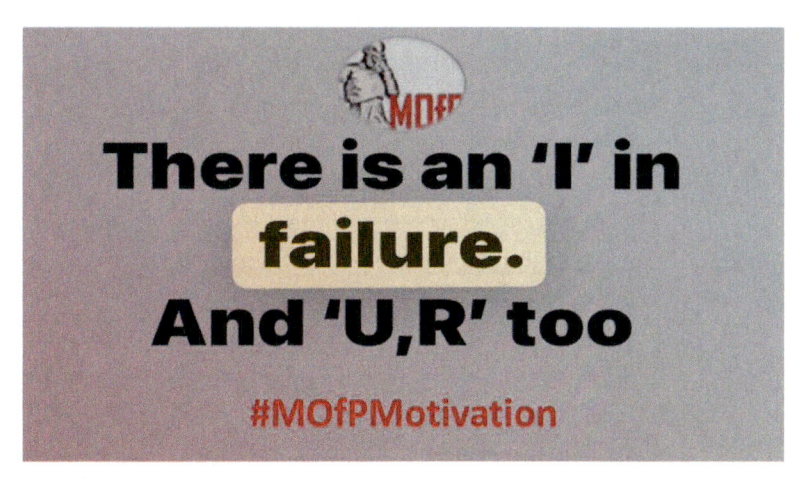

#MOfPMotivation

Figure 15 - Failure - always an option, whatever they tell you

The Strategy of 'Lessness'

In all museums, galleries and heritage sites (as indeed most activities in the world), we need our teams to focus on delivering more.

At MOfP we have developed a strategy that is so advanced it encompasses everything we need our teams to do, in such a way they are unaware that we are, essentially delivering a long con.

Our 'Do more, with less, more often, more efficiently, with a lower budget and with greater enthusiasm', neatly encompasses all elements of what we need our staff to do.

We need teams to:

- Deliver our ever-increasing exhibition and live activity programmes hitting an increasingly diverse audience and driving greater income.
- Deliver this with fewer staff, less budget, less time, less training and less investment, in colder and darker spaces.
- Deliver the programme 7-days a week, extend the operating window so we do pre-opening events, post opening events, and sleepovers.
- Deliver this with 25% of the budget we would have had available in 2019 before the plague.
- Deliver everything with enthusiasm that hides the sheer levels of tiredness, general fatigue and stress. And give us a positive score in the latest staff survey.

So how to achieve this?

The answer is to shame people into feeling inadequate every time they fail to deliver way above and beyond what you could reasonably expect.

There are all kinds of ways you can do this as a manager. It's essential ideally to hit the sweet spot of maximum shaming in a positive and inclusive way.

This isn't a job this is a 'calling'

Your family don't like seeing you anyway - what have you got to lose?

If you don't do this good for wider society - who will?

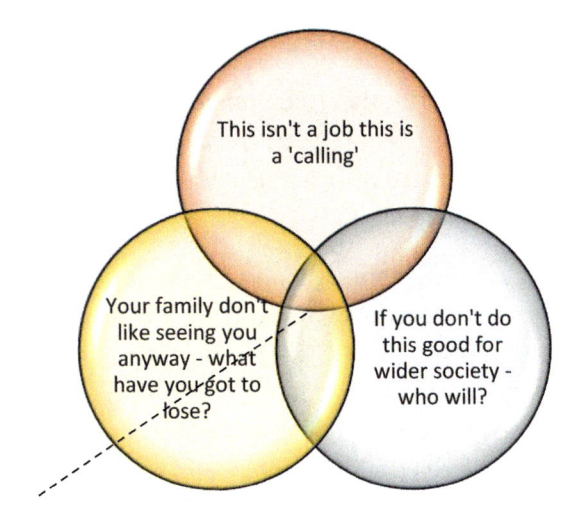

Maximum shame

Figure 16 - The point of maximum shame

The law of next year

It is possible that you will hear complaints when you implement the 'lessness' strategy, but this can be ignored by simply reminding all colleagues that it will be 'quieter next year'.

It will ALWAYS be quieter next year.

It will NEVER be quieter next year.

Face it, in 2020 you actually ended up closing for ages by law and it was busier without visitors than it was with them.

Understanding your senior teams

Here we turn our attention to the importance of understanding how senior teams think so that you are better equipped for the kinds of strategic decisions that you will be on the receiving end of.

A the point a senior team is planning important strategy it is vital they can think without the constraints of reality. This means the ideas, when they reach you, will need to be reinterpreted taking into account barriers such as gravity, human behaviour, budgets, and many other pesky elements that prevent the realisation of those prefect dreams.

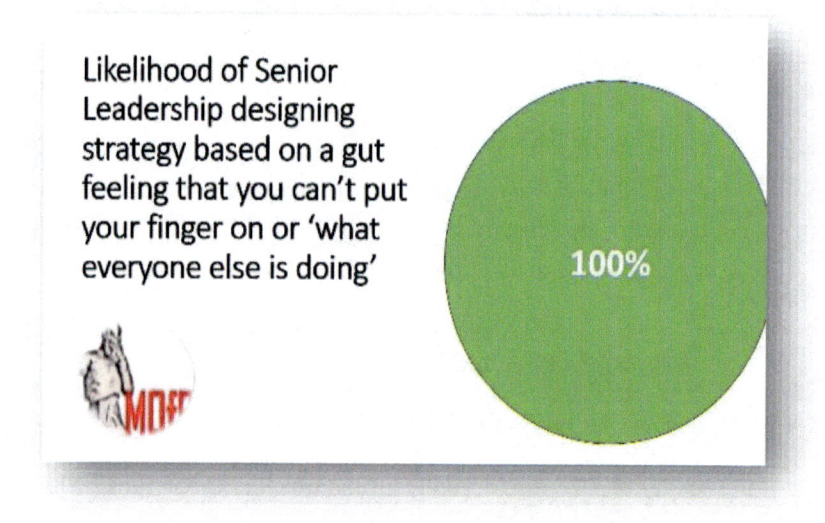

Figure 17 – Gut instinct matters

The clarity of ignorance

Although your senior team employs you, and many others, as experts in a particular field. The lack of knowledge they themselves hold means they are able to think, unclouded by factors which impinge upon your own planning. A knowledge of the current market, the way the museum works, or the visitor and staff reaction on the ground, should all be ignored so that appropriate emphasis can be place upon the gut feeling of a couple of more vocal members of the museum board, or even more annoyingly, what they've heard another museum they have no experience of is doing.

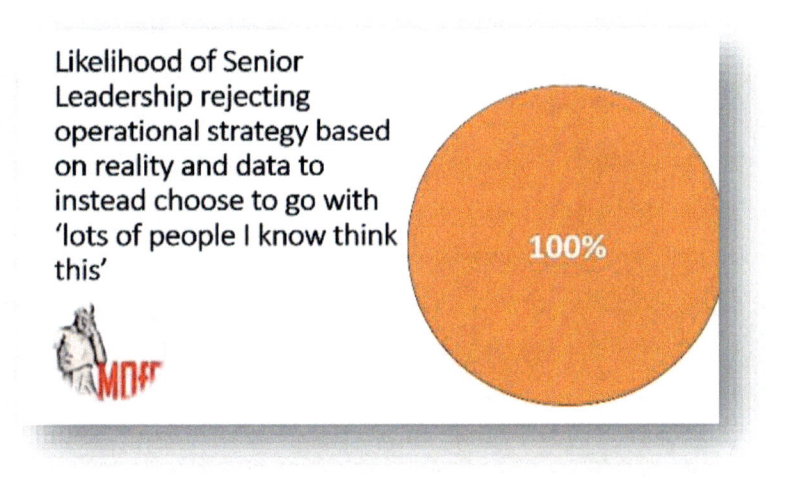

Likelihood of Senior Leadership rejecting operational strategy based on reality and data to instead choose to go with 'lots of people I know think this' — 100%

Figure 18 - operational reality should be ignored

The Knowable

Your Board were appointed because they are people who know things. They have had interesting and varied careers and now they support you. They know people, and not people like you know – important people who have opinions that matter. For that reason, all decisions will be made against any data or operational experience. Instead, the Board will talk to people they like talking to and use their insight to make those vital judgement calls. That's why they are who they are, and you will remain who you are, which is negligible.

Figure 19 - Think outside your organisation

Multi-organisational ghosting

It's frequently noted by the Directors at MOfP that 'the Head of X at Museum Y is doing Z'.

This never proves to be true. When you contact your friend, who actually is the aforementioned Head of X, they'll confirm that they have never even considered 'Z' because that would be insane. However, their boss, who is friends with your boss is super-keen on the idea.

All such conversations are best dealt with by politely nodding and saying that you will 'follow that up urgently'. You should then hope with all your heart that nothing comes of this.

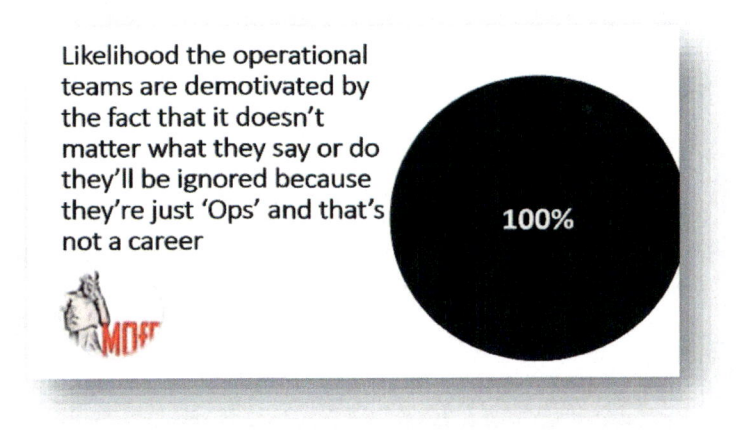

Figure 20 - Annoying your teams is key – operations is just a job, never a career

Careering off

The final element to consider, is who you are within the museum. If you work in the operational teams who actually deliver the experience to thousands of people a year, your opinion will not count.

This is because operational work, or work with visitors is not a career path. Operational work is what the nieces and nephews of Directors do for work experience when they are

14. If you are working in operations it must be assumed that this is an error on your part and that you would be better placed working in a department store, if only they still existed.

Assuming you are clear on the factors affecting the decision making process – we have left out the concept of 'dumb luck' as we take that for granted – we can now consider what is known to front of house teams as the 'excitement gap'.

Mind the Gap

We've all been there.

The grand reveal for the programme for the year ahead is announced to the team. There's a pregnant silence, someone near the back coughs and a number of colleagues check their online diary in case it's April 1st.

It isn't April 1st.

That exhibition featuring envelope types from the 1950's, and sponsored by one of the Trustees is going to be the cornerstone of the Autumn programme. And it isn't going to be going postal.

The diagram below illustrates what we call **'the excitement gap'**.

Figure 21 - The excitement gap

Once the programme has been signed off it will fall to other teams to limp on and try to deliver the expected visitor numbers.

Visitor numbers will have been generated either using a random number generator, or by the Trustees looking at the initial proposal and insisting that's doubled.

There are a number of ways to salvage this terrible decision on the part of the Board.

- Promote the exhibition more. This is a double-edged sword, it could be that people hear more about it and that puts them off. You'll just have to take the chance.
- Activate the exhibition. This is really easy and cheap to do because front of house staff are never doing anything

anyway. You can encourage teams to tell interesting stories about the exhibition, if there are none then it's best to go off at a tangent and talk about something else.
- Curatorial tours. You could run some of these. However, if the exhibition was foisted on the curators by the Board, it's likely they're as pissed off as the rest of the organisation so this will end up being painful to arrange and attend.
- Just close it.
- Check the insurance policy for the museum. Once you're confident you have sufficient cover, set a fire.

Part 3

It's all about them

Chapter 7

Operating a museum
'Visitors won't ever do that'.

A quote from almost every curator at MOfP

The invisibility cloak.

It's a truth seldom admitted that every museum, gallery, or heritage attraction has many ways of finding out what visitors actually think.

Although front of house staff are seldom seen by much of the rest of the organisation, it's curious that they seem to be pretty heavily involved in many day-to-day visitor interactions.

It's fair to say that if visitors come into your museum, they're more likely to meet either a member of the front of house team, or even a volunteer, rather than one of those people you see on fly-on-the wall shows on Channel 5 about what it's like to work in a museum if you're the nephew of the Chair of the Trustees.

Whilst invisible to back of house staff, it's worth considering if front of house staff may actually be of value to your operation.

Museum Operations

An Introduction

MOfP was originally set up to retain and explain the many failed efforts of front of house teams to get the rest of the organisation to understand what running a museum would actually be like if you took into consideration the following elements of experience.

1) Visitors
2) Collections
3) Everything else

As these concepts are generally not considered together we'll take some time to examine them here.

1) Visitors

Later in Chapter 12 we will be considering our audiences (even those we don't want). Visitors are unfortunately necessary in order to maintain a museum. We realise that this is hugely problematic for many members of the museum community. If you take some time to consider the average variety of visitors to your most recently curated display, it will be clear that many of them are not the kind of people we were hoping for when we went into this business. It is, sadly, impossible to force visitors to read every single piece of interpretation, to take a basic test at the end of a visit in order to establish that learning objectives have been met, or to be sufficiently grateful for the work we have done to educate them. Instead, we still find many visitors come to our spaces expecting to have a 'good time', 'meet friends' or even just to 'avoid the cold'. It is to be hoped that the continued rise of virtual reality, theme parks and streaming services will reduce visitor numbers.

2) Collections

The collection is clearly the only reason the museum exists. Whilst it's essential to curatorial colleagues that our visitors appreciate that we have in our collection the 13th best example of a rococo coffee table in the world, and one of the lesser known original transcripts of a McGonagall poem, our visitors are generally not interested.

The fact that collections care colleagues have shrouded everything in darkness making it impossible to see, and plunged the display spaces into temperatures that require all visitors to wear mittens (for reasons of relative humidity), makes it seven more challenging to promote deeper engagement.

3) Everything else

Can we be honest with you? It's the 'everything else' that's a major concern. Whilst we don't like to invest in toilets, queueing systems, ticketing systems, lighting, general routine maintenance, major maintenance, upgrades to IT, staffing levels, improved café facilities and functioning doors – all of this is pretty important to our visitors and gets commented on more than the collection. This further highlights the clear learning from many years of Museum operation. Visitors are either idiots, or they're idiots. Until a new business plan is developed, they do remain a necessity.

Does your museum have a visitor facing team?

Before we delve further into the mysteries of how your museum operates. We want you to take a moment and consider something. Does your museum have a front house team?

You may call them 'Visitor Services' (they probably haven't called themselves since the late 1980's), perhaps they're 'Customer Services', 'Operations' (they aren't called that, it's just what they sigh and say when you fail to remember their departmental name in a meeting. Again), 'Visitor Operations'? 'Visitor Experience'? or maybe just 'them'?

At MOfP we have a Visitor Experience team. So, we're going to call them that. You can continue to call them whatever it is you like. You do you.

What do they even do?

There is a very simple way of understanding what a member of staff in a Visitor Experience team does.

We simply need to apply the Triple 'T' Test.

Ask yourself this basic question.

'Is it tricky, tedious or terrifying?'

If you can answer yes to any of these then the project or work area you are dealing with should be handed straight over to operational colleagues.

In order to demonstrate this approach fully we have included a number of case studies below and a simple flow chart to help you through the 'delegation' process.

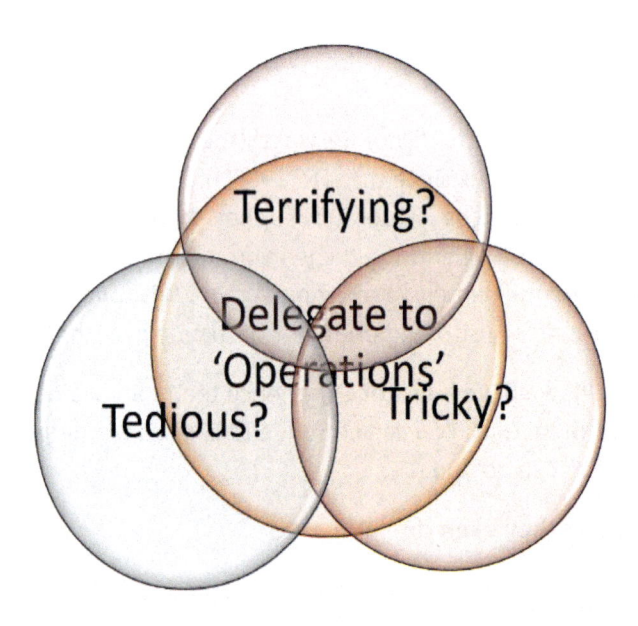

Figure 22 - The Triple 'T' Test

CASE STUDY ONE

You are about to embark on a major new exhibition.

Everything within it has been designed bespoke. Large numbers of the public are expected to attend.

The items on show are hugely controversial and will lead to much negative press, as well as a range of safeguarding issues for the team.

The main interactive area includes a firework making activity for under 5's and the introduction of naked flames in the area of a loan item which the government indemnity scheme has refused to cover.

The budget is tiny and all staff costs have already been removed from the programme budget.

What should you do?

This is simple. You should find the Head of Operations and make them responsible for delivering this project. You should work closely with PR to prepare a line to use in all relevant media articles when the inevitable happens and send the Head of Operations on a media training workshop.

A clear audit trail should be developed which implicates the Head of Operations in all key decisions.

If all goes well a Director or Senior Curator should step in and take all the credit for the excellent delivery of this era defining moment.

CASE STUDY TWO

A Major gala dinner is being delivered in the museum this evening. The client is exceptionally demanding and keeps moving the goal posts. The Operations team have already worked hard with all other teams on delivering a plan to manage visitor access during the day and balance this with the event but the client wants more.

What should you do?

Essentially, the less the Operations team know, the less they'll stick their oar in. You know them, always after a risk assessment, a safe working plan, an evacuation plan, a staffing plan, and a management strategy for looking after the collection in our care.

Cut them out of the loop.

Do what the client wants.

If it all goes pear-shaped, throw the Duty Manager and the operations team under the bus.

TRICKY?
TERRIFYING?
TEDIOUS?

Figure 23 - Tricky, Tedious, Terrifying? Our constant refrain in operations

But where are they?

We' assume the operations team frequently fail to attend the meetings you set up to discuss important new projects.

Here are some simple mistakes people make when setting up meetings involving front of house colleagues (the ones who actually run the place)

1) **Scheduling meetings at precisely the time the museum opens** to the public. Can you imagine why this might be

problematic for your colleagues, if there job is LITERALLY, to open the museum at the time you choose to meet?

2) **Failing to invite front of house colleagues** – after all, aside from knowing our visitors, how our site works, and what the visitor flow, numbers and feedback is, what can they contribute?

3) **Moaning that front of house colleagues don't show up.** Where could they be? Ah, perhaps they are staffing the exhibition that you recently opened and handed over to them, and which they will be managing for the next year whilst you start on the next one. Perhaps they are coping with all the numerous issues you failed to consider when designing that last exhibition and have less 'free time' as a result?

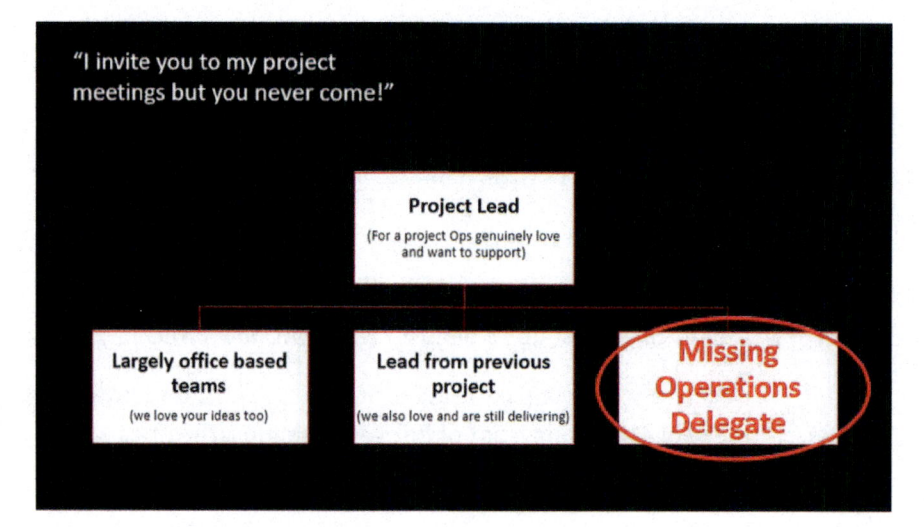

Figure 24 - Missing delegate syndrome

Project Creep

It's universally acknowledged that a large part of the role of Operations teams is (like all teams) dealing with things that nobody originally expected to be part of the project.

A key difference for operations teams is that they are the single point of contact with visitors in many cases.

It is highly likely that the visitor will be better equipped with knowledge of the latest changes to a particular experience, than the team who are charged with delivering it.

Figure 25 shows the most common progression from pre to post opening.

The '**Four points of expectation**' cover the main areas which teams expect to be delivered. These are always agreed in advance.

Typically, in a gallery or museum environment this includes.

- Security – because someone has to make sure things don't get stolen or licked.
- Customer Service – because we like to try to be nice to people.
- Health and Fire Safety – because a living visitor is a repeat visitor.
- Engagement activity – because we know engagement and immersion are vital, but we also know that they are usually an after-thought and have not been built into the original project. Or they were built into the original project but cut because everyone couldn't believe how much people actually cost to employ.

The final point is a real point of contention. Everyone wants it – visitors, staff, grant providers. Nobody wants to pay for it. The operations team will therefore deliver everything at short notice and without the relevant training and support. As a result, it will suck more than it was supposed to.

The four points of extrapolation

The next stage in the model covers how the initial tacit agreements stretch when confronted with reality.

1. Unexplained and tricky loan agreements – this is when the curator reveals that they only got the star object by agreeing to 3 staff within a 23.5cm vicinity of the object. Two of them should have superpowers. One needs to be the actual Batman.
2. A late handover – It didn't get finished on time, but that's fine. Operations teams love nothing more than learning on the job, right? Even better if they are learning during the Press view, they're supposed to be managing.
3. Inventory checks – 'Just check it's all there'. It's not difficult. Except when you don't have the lists ready for the teams to check because they didn't get finalised in a timely fashion.
4. Another random afterthought – Maybe it's a festival of activity around the exhibition that just popped into the Director's head the day we opened. Maybe it's a complete change to the visitor routes? Perhaps you'd

just like all the staff to juggle and sing while looking after the space? All good. Of course.

Figure 25 again, highlights this constant 'evolution' in action.

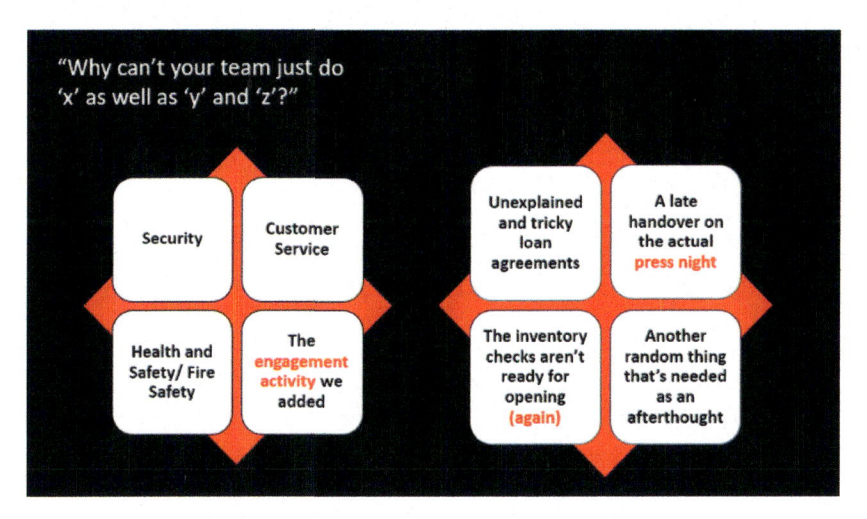

"Why can't your team just do 'x' as well as 'y' and 'z'?"

| Security | Customer Service | | Unexplained and tricky loan agreements | A late handover on the actual press night |
| Health and Safety/ Fire Safety | The engagement activity we added | | The inventory checks aren't ready for opening (again) | Another random thing that's needed as an afterthought |

Figure 25 - The points of expectation move towards extrapolation

Customer Service

Presumably you go shopping, maybe you eat out on occasion. Perhaps the ticket office at your local opera house, or your chauffeur, ensure that you receive the service you require.

You have to wonder how they deliver this? And, given the lack of time and investment museums and galleries actually put into customer service training, you have to assume most Executive Boards think that great service happens by accident.

Customer service is such a dirty word in many museums, that we prefer to talk loudly of our 'visitors', 'stakeholders' or 'audiences' at every turn. God forbid we might consider there is any filthy transaction that takes place where we acquire income in return for 'service'.

What are our visitors doing in the shop? Simply acquiring knowledge and cultural capital.

What are our visitors doing in the café? Simply reflecting on the learning goals, they have targeted as part of their mind-expanding experience.

What are our visitors doing who paid for an exhibition ticket? They're not consumers at all, these people are supporting our work through their selfless act of philanthropy.

All of the above mean that there is never any need to consider what 'Service style' or 'Commercial approach' might be taken.

Smile Like You Mean It

In 2022 MOfP adopted a much more focussed approach, but as we are a museum, failed to invest in any actual training to ensure that the way our teams acted in the galleries, bore any relationship to the much vaunted values and mission statement our senior teams espouse at international conferences.

'SLUM it'

'SLUM it' is the result of our extensive under-investment and 'soft' focus on service.

Smile

Like

U

Mean

it

Figure 26 - Smile Like You Mean it

We were able to simply take an anthem first delivered at a Killers concert our Head of Visitor Experience had attended and play it on repeat throughout our galleries outside all visitor hours. Thus, all our front of house team are inculcated with the refrain 'Smile Like You Mean It'

This has the double effect of leading to most staff zoning out of any future training (saving us further investment), and of allowing colleague to appear genuinely pleased to see visitors.

Recruitment

We are all aware recruitment in museums is challenging. This is for a combination of reasons but most of all it is our ongoing ability to let ourselves off the hook with the usual excuses that maintain a consistent lack of diversity.

The usual entry route, like any other industry, is volunteering.

Which of us hasn't volunteered to fill shelves in our local supermarket? To deliver takeouts for free in our neighbourhood, to offer free taxi services to those commuters arriving off the last train, or to support hedge-fund managers by carrying their coffees.

No, there's nothing strange in the approach museums take to launching a career.

In recent years there has been much talk in the sector about how we can deliver improvements. Whether that is through more recognition of experience outside the form of a PhD, offering roles that are not gate-kept with unfathomable language, or even reaching out to new pools of talent who may previously not have seen us as a welcoming sector in which to work.

It's largely been talk.

Chapter 8

The Visitor Journey
'We all on a journey'…. Quotes from the pop stars.

We are all journeying here.

The visitor journey is an essential part of every discussion that takes place where strategy, direction and income is discussed. However, for many in the organisation it remains a complete puzzle.

For them the visitor journey is very much based on a process which begins with a complimentary ticket for all the latest exhibitions and ends with a warm glass of wine and a conversation with other people who work in the same bubble… and then on to the next opening event.

At MOfP we deliver a journey that is far more aligned to the experience of a visitor who isn't a good friend of the curator or someone who makes their income through questionable investments and therefore gets their name on the side of the building (until an unknowable future date when the reality of the source of funding becomes clear and press statements are followed by the hurried removal of the 'no-longer-entirely-appropriate' demarcation).

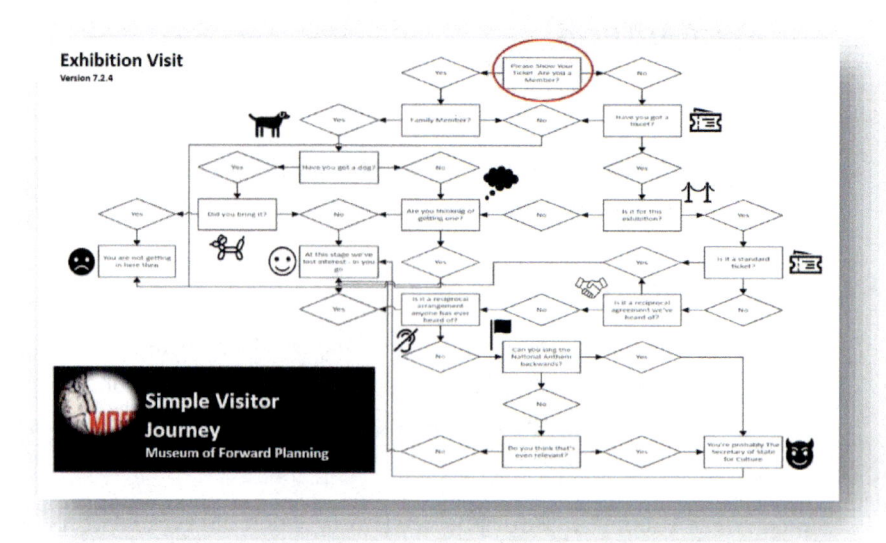

Figure 27 - A simple visitor journey

It is essential to remember that a visitor journey is not simply the onsite experience. You need to ensure that the experience is consistent at all key touch-points.

Museums need to ensure that every other interaction comes down to the same level as the weakest link in this chain so that we do not over-promise on the experience itself.

Consider a museum that has chosen to embrace cutting-edge technology such as cups on string to enable the set-up of a new-fangled call centre, or the ability to purchase a ticket in advance so it can be posted out to visitors before they even reach the museum itself!

If you then let the visitor down through failing to light the gas lamps in a timely fashion the whole experience becomes poorer and the variation will grate on your audience.

The offsite experience is, in every sense, *'out of sight, out of mind'* and as a result we can leave that to other teams to consider and the Executive team to decide not to invest in (after all we purchased a new ticketing system in 1997 so we don't want to over-invest in the key system which generates over 70% of our income).

A major element in any project is the need to deliver a consistent look and feel across the entire museum experience. Nobody will take responsibility for this, and although Visitor Experience will attempt to promote the idea, day-to-day it will be ignored entirely as the museum delivers a patchwork of siloed projects. Periodically there will be a commitment to change this approach, which will fade rapidly when faced with the reality of making the dull things work, like movement spaces between shiny new exhibitions, the toilets between shiny new exhibitions and the lifts required to take people between the shiny new exhibition spaces.

Onsite Challenges

This brief booklet can only hope to touch on a few of the key fundamentals of managing an operation on a daily basis, and the steps you must take to deliver for every visitor, even Members.

What we can do is cover a few of the essentials

Orientation and signage

We so often get the basics wrong. Signage can be the source of much amusement, as well as hopefully occasionally useful to both staff and visitors.

The best approach is that espoused by Ace of Base, in their seminal work on Museum signage.

Reflecting on their visit to a museum in 1993 'The Base' delivered this insight, which should sit in the hearts and minds of Operational managers everywhere.

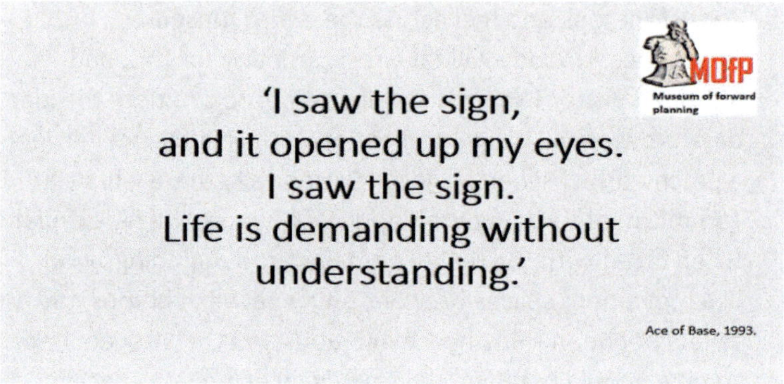
MOfP
Museum of forward planning
'I saw the sign,
and it opened up my eyes.
I saw the sign.
Life is demanding without
understanding.'
Ace of Base, 1993.

Figure 28 - Ace of Base dispense their wisdom on signage

'The Base' (as they were known amongst their Museum Studies cohort) were clear here on the transformative power of a decent sign. At MOfP we have taken this a step further and we apply the simple flow chart at figure 29 in all signage decision making.

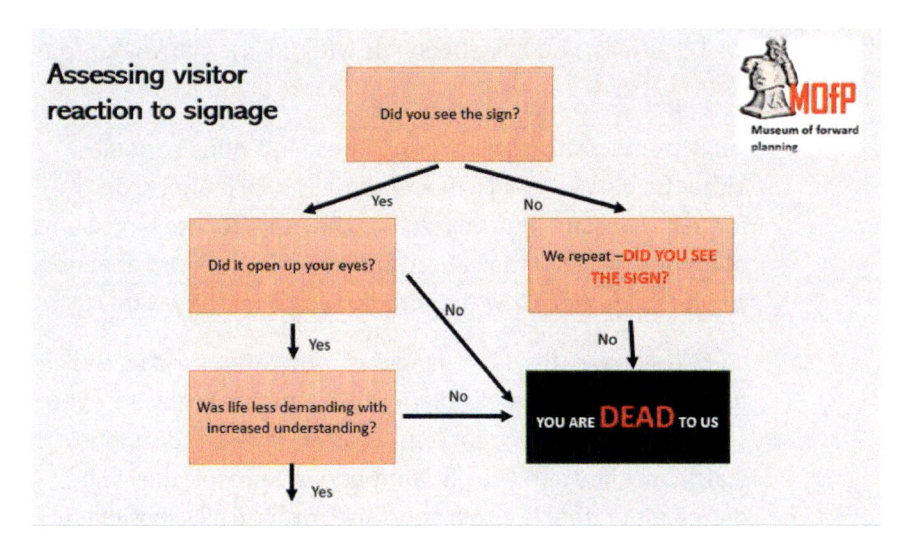

Figure 29 - The Base - Our signage strategy

It can be frustrating when visitors fail to see the signs, a number of key processes can be implemented to ensure there is more likelihood the sign will be both observed and acted upon.

1. Produce multiple copies of the same sign.
2. Place multiple copies of the same sign adjacent to each other in large groups.
3. Produce additional temporary signs, these should be laminated and pinned to a wall or collection object at a rakish angle.

If the visitor still chooses to ignore the sign.

4. Reproduce the sign, this time using red ink to print key details.
5. Add additional explanation marks.

If all else fails, you have been left with no alternative but to **CAPITALISE ALL SIGNAGE AND PRINT IN BOLD RED LETTERS.**

Sadly, some visitors will still fail. These individuals should either be ejected in a calm and professional manner, or forced to become Patrons so that they can donate large sums of money to the organisation, and we can therefore abandon all principles and allow them to do whatever they want.

'Subtle signage' this is an invidious term often used by design teams in museums and galleries. It means that they accept a sign is needed (maybe for legal reasons, maybe to support staff), but they don't really want one. As a result they will design a sign that is either too small, or basically invisible. This will necessitate the application of multiple laminated signs in order to rectify a problem which had already been identified.

Signage examples

The issue with subtle signage is that it does not 'cut it'. Visitors should be made to read the signage, understand the signage and obey the signage. Do not pull your punches, if you do, they will sense your weakness and strike. Then where will we all be?

Figure 30 and 31 - Some examples of effective signage

Figure 32 - Sometimes we can be too subtle

Myth Busting

There are many myths about running a modern museum. How and why do things go wrong? It cannot be the over-stretched teams, and ever reducing budgets.

Rather than beat about the bush, we simply share here the main culprits of our many and varied failures in recent pieces of work.

Museum Myths

The Signage Imp

Sometimes signs don't work as intended. Perhaps the icon that looked fine in design now resembles something phallic? Maybe the directional arrows point the wrong way?

If a forest of signs appears, all of which confuse the visitors and staff, and which nobody claims responsibility for – you have a signage imp.

Glorying in the use of drawing pins, lamination pouches and multiple fonts, the signage imp aims to help by USING CAPS LOCK and adding MORE signs.

Figure 33 - The signage imp

Museum Myths

Barrier Banshee and Cone Orc

While the Tensa Fairy creates mayhem with the Satie barriers, the harrowing cries of the Head of Visitor Experience are most frequently heard when the Barrier Banshee and Cone Orc crews have been at work.

Areas of the site that have been repaired and are now safe will be found festooned with warning signs and barriers, creating mystical pentagrams that summon further 'once wet floor' signage to the central point of magic.

Figure 34 - The barrier banshee and cone orc

Museum Myths

The Barrier Fairie

Was your museum built on a fairy ring? It's more than likely.

Despite warnings to architects that the little folk must be respected (which does explain some of the more bizarre museum layouts), those of us who work in areas that once held fairy kingdoms are well acquainted with the acts of enchantment involving tensa barriers.

Random layouts, moving barriers, or queueing systems that turn in on themselves so visitors are lost forever, locked in a mysterious and never ending 'wait time'. Beware the fairie folk.

Figure 35 - The barrier faerie

Museum Myths

The Typo Troll

Lurking in printer cartridges, the typo troll ensures that every new exhibition has at least one blindingly obvious typo.

Despite numerous checks by colleagues – at the very moment of opening on Membership Day, the typos will appear. It is rumoured the troll is the spirit of a past visitor who loved the museum but would always take pride in finding the one 'tiny error', now trapped by the magical font fairies for eternity.

Figure 36 - The typo troll

Barriers

Nobody understands barriers like front of house teams.

Much like 'subtle signage' barriers are often seen as the devil's work by teams who do not have to consider the devil is absolutely in the detail of managing visitor flow and crowd safety at a busy exhibition or museum site.

The constant removal of barriers means that the exact number onsite will remain, at all times, a mystery, any form of count or stocktake will be frustrated. Different museum teams hold wildly subjective views on barriers and their use:

Team	View on barriers
Security	They're absolutely essential for safe operation of our spaces and crowd control
Commercial Events	They're so essential for our events we will steal them all and store them where nobody else can find them
Visitor Experience	They're absolutely essential for safe operation of our space and customer service
Curatorial	They are the work of the devil, unnecessary and must be destroyed
Executive team	We've never seen a queue (there are no queues at opening events), so you don't need them
Finance	You've got LOADS of barriers, we are always seeing them
Schools team	Please get more barriers, we need to have a way to control them

There is nothing as exciting for a front of house manager, then being able to set up a new queuing system, and seeing it working seamlessly, even for weeks and years ahead.

There is nothing as heart breaking, as seeing a senior leader remove these barriers to create carnage and chaos in the place of order.

You only need to look at footage of the storming of the Capitol, 6th January 2019, to see that even at the height of the unrest, rioters respected the barriers that were in place.

The operations teams rest their case.

Figure 37 - Queue like nobody is watching

Workload

It's a truth universally acknowledged by anyone who has never worked in operational teams, that staff just appear at will and can work for endless hours without the need for breaks and operating 24 hours a day, 7 days a week.

Staffing budgets are always massive in operational teams, it's as if they have loads of people. Clearly someone somewhere is pulling a fast one.

'Voluntary' overtime is of course the answer. If you've ever worked in a team that delivers the 'day job' of opening and operating a museum 7 days a week, and then runs events and activities each evening and morning out of hours you will appreciate the 'funnel of plenty'. This is the result of the brilliant creativity of numerous teams which delivers a wide array of programming and activities to the operations team... for them to ... deliver.

As one creative team finishes their project and goes off for a well-earned rest and a round of (never to be read) washup reports and meetings, the next creative team launches their activity on an unsuspecting operations team.

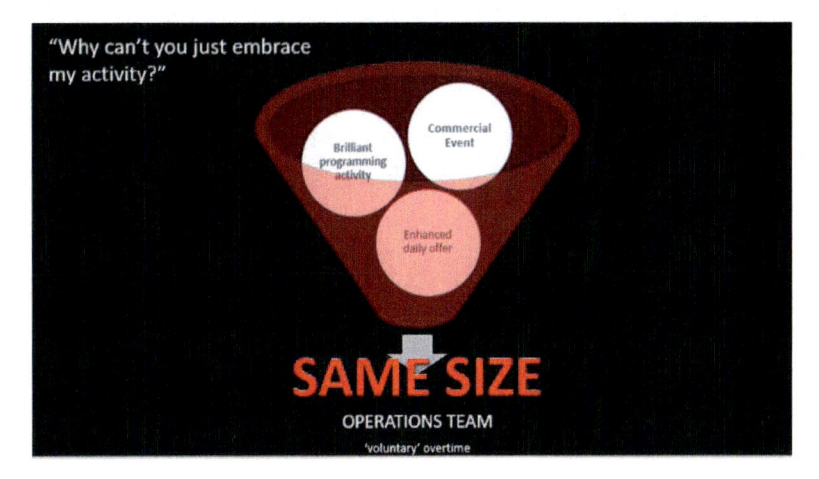

Figure 38 - The infinity horn

Working the white elephant

If you work in #operations you know that architects do not. You have possibly worked with the same practices time and again. Each time they have made the same errors. Rather than examine the detail of the pain here, we will be looking at the operational obstacles presented in building design in chapter 16 in much more detail.

We have covered some of the elements that are key to day-to-day visitor journey. As this is the core of everything we do, and the main experience for most people onsite, we do not need to give them any further consideration. This will certainly be the case for the Museum Board, who only ever attend major new openings of our exhibitions. Like moths drawn to warm white wine and those weird rice-crackers.

We will now move on to the only part of any site that matters. The temporary exhibition.

Chapter 9

The Museum Exhibition

Conception

Our museum looks through the lens of the front of house teams. For this reason, exhibition design is not really our area of expertise. As any curator knows, front of house teams just ask difficult questions and point out design flaws. If this approach fails they actively coach visitors to ensure that the design flaws they mentioned come true.

In most cases an exhibition must be conceived with as little though as possible to the impact that visitors will have upon it. If we allow this to intrude on the design, we are effectively 'dumbing down', assuming that visitors cannot understand the complexities and intricacies of what we present. While this may be a valid assumption, and the knowledge gatekeeping we want to perpetuate as a curatorial team, it's best to pretend otherwise except when in the company of fellow academic

There are some key areas to cover in exhibition design, but it seems best to start with basics as nobody ever does. The following questions are dull but really quite important:

1.. How big is the space you are sticking the stuff in?

2. How many people do you want to see the stuff?

3. Is the stuff delicate?

4. Do you need people to look after the stuff?

5. Do you want visitors to enjoy looking at the stuff or do you not give a toss?

Flow and capacity

So, let's start with the first couple of points, and lose the will to live from there onwards

In the unlikely event a menial/member of the front of house team makes it into a design meeting, they will undoubtedly want to raise concerns that the spaces allocated to the major blockbuster exhibition will not accommodate the sheer volume of visitors that everyone is expecting to attend.

This will, of course, be questioned by the lead curator. A model response to this discussion is shown below.

Curator: 'Are you sure we can't fit 25,998 people through this 2 metre square room per day?'

FOH: 'Are you sure that the research you've presented as the centrepiece to this exhibition is valid?'

Curator: 'Well of course'

FOH: 'Touché'

This is a conversation you will need to endlessly repeat.

Staffing and stuff

The exhibition will always require more staffing than the museum has budget to afford. Let's examine why this is.

1. Nobody realises that staff have to be there 7 days a week if the museum is open 7 days a week.
2. Nobody realises that real humans need a break and may need the toilet. So you need more people than you drew on the plan (if you even drew people).
3. The staffing cost is seldom the problem of the exhibition designer – they'll be gone when that particular bill lands.
4. Nobody ever really considers the loan agreement they just signed off might have implications in the real, actual world.

Let's assume (outlandishly) that as an exhibition is usually largely made up of stuff the museum usually doesn't have on display or own (leaving aside the fact that most of the collection it owns it maybe stole) and it will be no surprise to anyone other than the entire project team – that the stuff in the exhibition is delicate and needs a lot of looking after.

Visitors

Imagine the exhibition is going to be visited by real people. Not just people who like museums / live in museums / run museums or curate museums – this can actually happen!

Now try and imagine they don't understand all the stuff you have on the walls, all the language you've used and all the detail and learning points you have crammed into your life work – which for them is the 35-40 minutes before the café.

How could you help people understand?

Maybe you could share all the stuff you know with the front of house teams that will be in the space and maybe they will then tell the visitors. Clearly, this is just a thought.

Reverse Exhibition Bingo

If you don't work front of house, then the exhibition only exists for you before it launches, on the opening night when it all seems brilliant, and then in the pesky wash-up meeting where the front of house teams whinge needlessly.

To save you the bother we've put together a bingo card that can be used to review progress at all project meetings – and can act as a detailed report which can be filed with the others.

Reverse Bingo – Exhibition Design
After the project meeting tick off what wasn't considered important!

Visitor Flow through the space	That small font size that isn't workable	The lack of contrast between the floor and the plinths
Still no final details on staffing positions	Still no agreement on whether there's a leaflet	That pinch point that's been designed in
There isn't enough light to read the interpretation	There's too much light for conservation	The merchandise is crap as the image rights weren't agreed (again)

Figure 39 - The exhibition design card

Some key points to consider.

This will fall on deaf ears, but it is worth writing some words down in the hope someone, somewhere, somehow takes them in.

Access

Almost every exhibition design will, until the last minute, include an immersive experience that is really hard to explain or understand for the front of house teams but will be utterly transformative and brilliant. This will actually happen sometimes.

It's important to note that there is very little chance the experience will be fully accessible. It's likely to include bright lights, loud music and at least one area that requires a ramp which cannot be installed for reasons of aesthetic appearance.

It is the role of the Visitor Experience teams to point this out extensively so that when the inevitable complaints come in, the Visitor Experience team are prepared to defend what they know is indefensible, and to take the rap for not designing an inclusive and accessible visitor experience – which they did not design but had forced upon them by people who told them 'that won't happen'.

It's not 'quirky' it's unthinkingly inaccessible

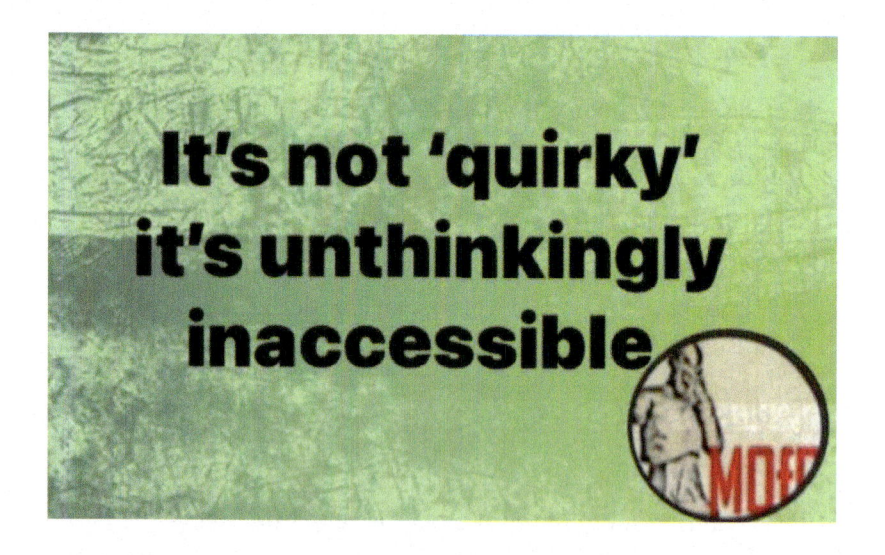

Visitor Feedback

As figure 39 below, shows, there is always a group of well-intentioned people in an office somewhere who want to know what visitors think. It is likely that there is a group of well-intentioned people in the exhibition space who know precisely what people think.

Like oil and water these two must never be permitted to mix.

Instead, we suggest calling in a consultancy company who can review your exhibition and report back at length that everything was brilliant, just like you planned.

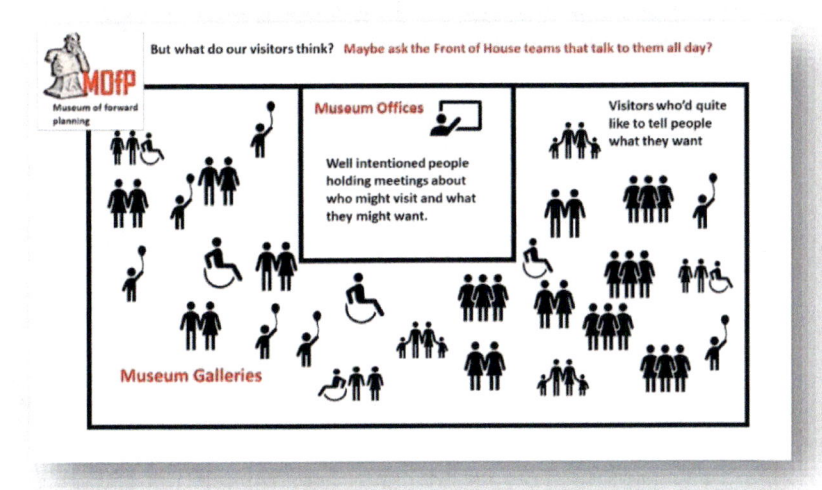

Figure 40 - If only we could find some visitors to talk to

Realism in the future

It's easy to poke fun at exhibitions, but we all know that the paid exhibition is the lifeblood of many museums, and the closest thing to an actual business model we have. So, it has to be made to work.

Perhaps the main issue (as we will see in later chapters) is that Marketing and PR teams simply over-promise.

One potential solution is that we instead, offer a realistic approach to exhibition layout and design and that we incorporate many of the essential failings at an early stage, rather than retrofitting them when the exhibition is already half way to being closed with dwindling visitation and almost negative dwell times.

Key highlights for all exhibitions need to be:

- Themed tensator barriers to ensure there is some sort of visitor flow throughout.
- An area for immersive technological interaction but where the network connection is lost.
- An area that is underwhelming because the projector bulb needs to be replaced and the budget is spent.
- An area with an array of signage indicating that the fault is important, and an engineer has been called.
- A spacious area to 'decompress' which is actually sparce because we ran out of budget in the earlier stages of design.
- If we can agree on this, more rigid, design focus. We can be sure to achieve our desired outcomes more fully.

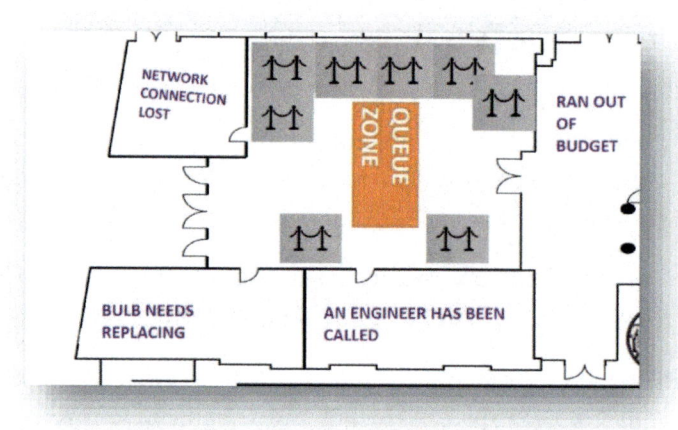

Figure 41 - A more realistic exhibition design approach

Chapter 10

Collection responsibility

Why does your museum even exist? Before there was a mission statement and a vision, before there were values and practices, it's likely that, in the UK at least, your museum exists because a very rich, and ethically questionable Victorian industrialist had enough money and chutzpah to collect many important items from around the world as if they belonged to him. And it was him.

The statue of your founder is now confined to the area in the corner of the museum next to the sign that indicates you, as an institution, are sorry for the numerous crimes against people, freedoms, the sanctity of long-held faiths, the destruction of complex societal structures, and the general pillaging of the colonies the individual claimed to be civilising. Your Board aren't sorry enough to make that statement any more boldly, and to be fair if they did, they would be pilloried in every daily paper except for the Guardian.

But you have a collection and that matters, because you wouldn't exist without it.

Collection matters

The issue with the collection is that it is free for all visitors to see, and as such nobody has any interest in it from an institutional perspective. It won't get the attention and support of the desperately needed exhibitions which raise the income for the organisation.

It won't attract stacks of visitors – although there will be one key item that everyone comes to see all the time. Whatever the curatorial team attempt to do to highlight other items, it will make no difference. Embrace the fact everyone wants to see Lady Doxley's Fan. It is all you have.

Collections essentially 'anti-matter', although they are all around us, although we would not exist without them, they do not exist in the eyes of the Trustees – other than on postcards. Have we mentioned that at least one Trustee always wants more postcards?

As collections do not attract visitors and cannot be monetised (legally at any rate – the car boot sales we hold each month are legend at MOfP, but we would rather people continue to believe they are mythical), they are seen as a negative factor. They cost without return. And the damn things keep getting bigger.

The one hope for an item in the MOfP collection is that it will be loaned to another museum somewhere. This means it will immediately become the star of a show (presumably one the museum can charge for), as a result MOfP will demand all manner of protection, conservation and invigilation, when we all know the piece concerned usually languishes next to the old visitor toilet block that is no longer used because of the unfortunate smell.

The postcard at figure 41..

1) It's a damn postcard so the Trustees are happy

2) It explains the different views elements of the museum teams have of what exactly a museum is and therefore how much space it needs.

| Curatorial | Health and Safety | Trustees |
| Development | Membership | Collection Care |

Figure 42 - The museum, and how we see it

Fundamentally, it may be worth reflecting, it is more than possible that your founder was late to the party in terms of creating a museum. Perhaps all the good topics and themes were taken? Perhaps your museum is effectively just 'Miscellaneous items'. Doesn't mean you don't have to look after them though. Who knows what future generations might need? Plus, there's a high chance the people you stole it off may want it back.

Just because you collect it, doesn't mean it's interesting

Figure 43 - But is it worth looking at?

Collection cataloguing

There will be an issue with the cataloguing of your museum collection. Curators at various stages will have taken a frankly cavalier approach to recording and cataloguing the essential elements of the collection which they profess to care so much about. To be fair, the public will also have sabotaged the museum by donating huge amounts of tat which will consequently have been accidentally accessioned, along with the gift shop stock. Some of the gift shop stock is older than the collection in any case.

There are positives to be gleaned from this though.

It is only thanks to the process of badly cataloguing our collections, and thus annoying the Registrars who have been rightly demanding we 'do better' since the idea of a museum was first considered, that we are able to 'Discover' new things.

At this stage in the life-cycle of the planet, as we career towards an inevitable messy end, most things that are worth seeing have probably been seen. This may sound pessimistic, and it is.

However, we can 'Discover' things which everyone apart from the Registrar, Collections team, Audit team and Insurers, thought were lost, and for a fleeting moment we are therefore newsworthy and is may attract both free publicity and a few visitors too.

Inventory management

The final element of collection management (that we can be bothered to cover in this incomplete guide in any event), is ensuring the collection does not actually get taken away by visitors on a day-to-day basis.

This is an essentially easy task. After all, anyone with an iPad, wearing a name badge and a polo shirt, is absolutely properly equipped to prevent an international art heist on their own museum.

Let's assume though, that just occasionally things do go missing.

Maybe they go missing because they were actually scheduled to be removed, perhaps they are going on a long awaited loan? Maybe the team removing the piece forgets that they actually need to tell other teams they are moving it? Maybe they don't update any of the records that the front of house teams have to check every day?

This would of course, never happen, and nobody reading this will be nodding along with a sense of recognition and a memory of the sheer feeling of dread that settled in the pit of their stomach as they reviewed the CCTV with the Security team who had witnessed the item being removed by the collections team, but also inexplicably failed to consider it noteworthy.

If this ever happens to you, you will need to implement the 'Full Collins'.

The 'Full Collins' is a simple and effective way to remember the actions you need to take in the event that everyone is feeling a bit queasy and panicked and there is a likelihood of a major internal review of process, implementation and who actually gets to retain their job and the confidence of the Board*

*A top tip here, it's likely the Board will retain the confidence of the Board and the rest of you can whistle for it.

Figure 43 indicates the flowchart for implementing the 'Full Collins'

If you were born later than the mid-80's this won't be funny.

If you are reading the chapter on collections, you're just pleased someone remembered you exist.

PROBLEM SOLVING FLOWCHART

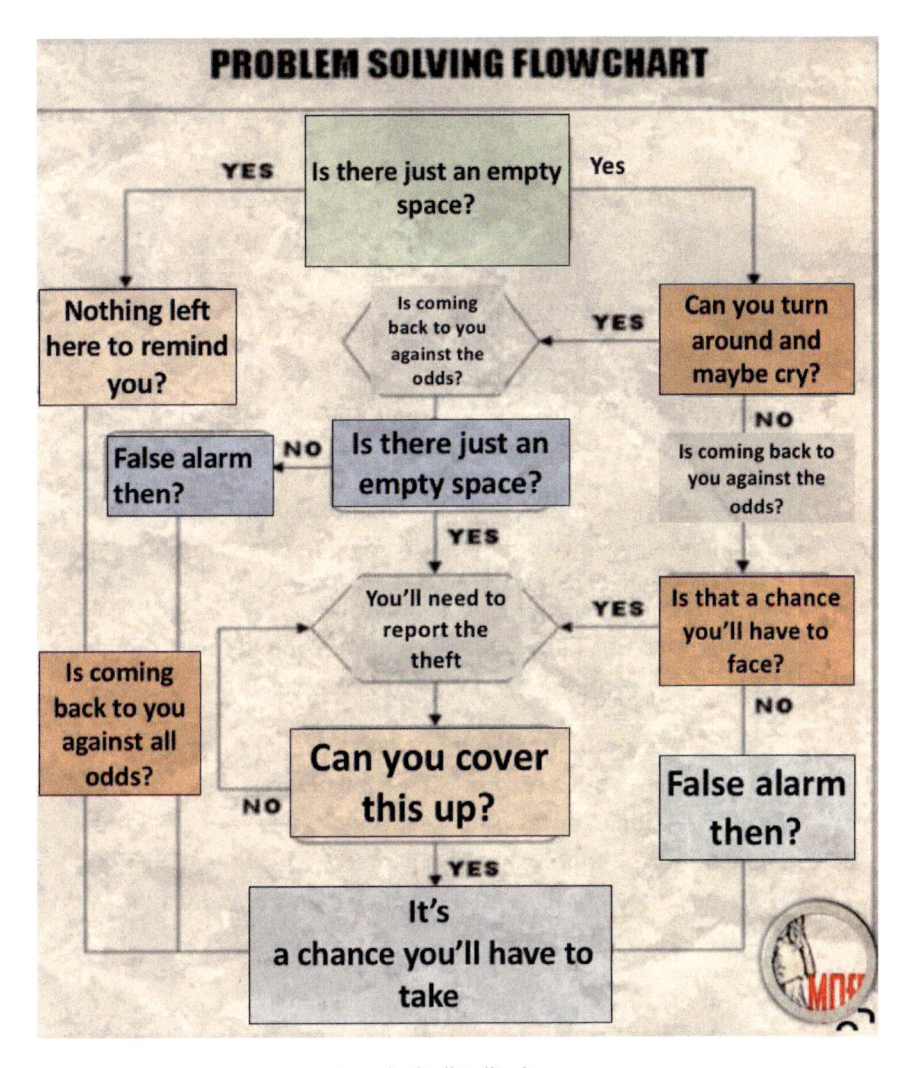

```
                    YES  ┌─────────────────┐  Yes
              ┌──────────│ Is there just an│──────────┐
              │          │  empty space?   │          │
              ▼          └─────────────────┘          ▼
     ┌─────────────┐      ┌─────────────┐      ┌─────────────┐
     │ Nothing left│      │  Is coming  │ YES  │Can you turn │
     │here to remind│     │ back to you │◄─────│ around and  │
     │    you?     │      │against the  │      │ maybe cry?  │
     └─────────────┘      │    odds?    │      └─────────────┘
                          └─────────────┘            │ NO
                                                     ▼
     ┌─────────────┐ NO   ┌─────────────┐      ┌─────────────┐
     │ False alarm │◄─────│Is there just an│   │Is coming back to│
     │   then?     │      │ empty space?│      │ you against the │
     └─────────────┘      └─────────────┘      │     odds?       │
                              │ YES            └─────────────┘
                              ▼                      │
                          ┌─────────────┐ YES  ┌─────────────┐
                          │You'll need to│◄────│Is that a chance│
                          │ report the  │     │you'll have to │
     ┌─────────────┐      │   theft     │     │    face?      │
     │ Is coming   │      └─────────────┘     └─────────────┘
     │back to you  │            │                   │ NO
     │against all  │            ▼                   ▼
     │   odds?     │      ┌─────────────┐      ┌─────────────┐
     └─────────────┘ NO   │Can you cover│      │ False alarm │
                   ──────│  this up?   │      │   then?     │
                          └─────────────┘      └─────────────┘
                              │ YES
                              ▼
                          ┌─────────────┐
                          │    It's     │
                          │a chance you'll have to│
                          │    take     │
                          └─────────────┘
```

Figure 44 - The 'Full Collins'

Chapter 11

Marketing

We all know how to do marketing. We've seen a poster, we love leaflets, we visited somewhere once. This makes every other person in the museum uniquely qualified to be judge all marketing collateral.

In this regard Marketing teams face the same challenges as operational teams. The fact what they do isn't valued as the expertise that it is.

The key deliverable for any Marketing team is to ensure the gap between the dream that is sold and the experience that is delivered remains at a constant.

Too much of a gap, and there will be complaints. If the gap is too little, there will be nothing to complain about.

Since our foundation MOfP has delivered a startling array of exhibitions which focus on the challenges associated with the intersection of curatorial dreams with operational nightmares. That inspirational interaction where a visitor comes into contact with our creative intent and responds on social media with '#WTF?!'

As Lux would have it

Tickets unavailable
#LowLuxSucks

Here we share just some of the numerous failures of recent years.

As Lux would have it -Collection care front and centre for once

We set out to challenge the widely held view from operational teams that light is necessary to enable visitors to see the collection, read the collection labels and enjoy themselves safely in any museum space.

An experience which was all delivered under the cloak of darkness, this enabled our conservation teams to bank the lux savings so we could later deliver out exhibition 'Flash, Bang, Wallop' about the impact of photography on the visitor experience.

W.T.F

Where's the Fun?

This exhibition picked up on the key learning objectives which focus groups of academics identified as the main aim of any visit for our unsuspecting families.

Devoid of any actual fun and accompanied by a family friendly café which consisted wholly of inedible health foods with all the fun and flavour sucked out due to an overdose of worthiness.

This dull but educational show failed to hit any attendance figures and was replaced with our soft-play area.

Key learning points for the team: Visitors are easily bored.

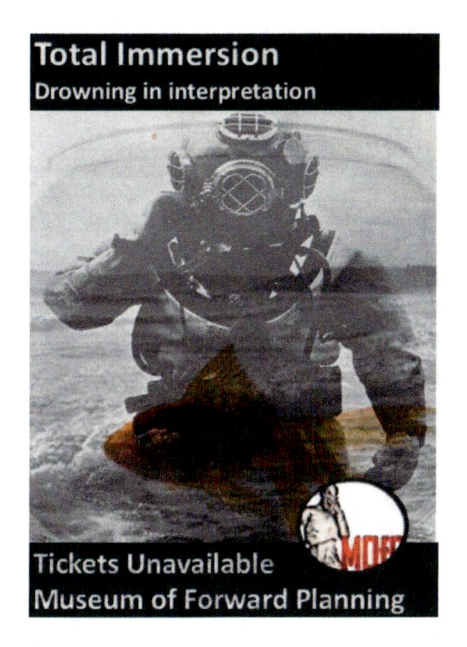

Total Immersion

Drowning in interpretation

Our short-lived experiment into binaural, virtual reality, dreamscape inspired, under-water exhibitions.

We took the idea of immersion to new heights /depths by flooding the museum galleries and issuing visitors with old fashioned diving gear so they found themselves 'swimming in history'.

A short-lived success.

People drowned.

Key learning points for the team: Keep the water in the buckets

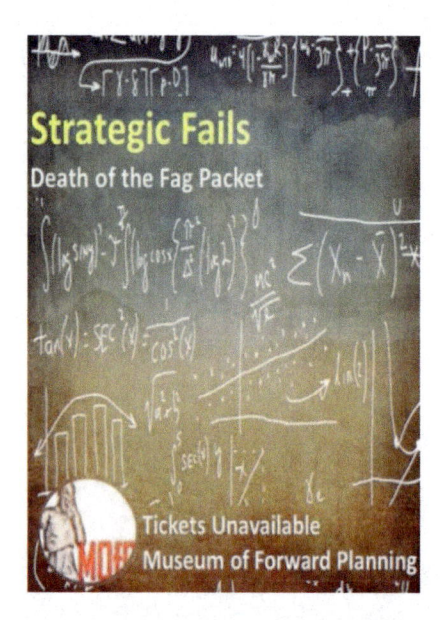

Strategic Fails

Death of the Fag Packet

This ground-breaking exhibition asked the important question – has the reduction in smoking led to the death of strategic planning?

Based on the thesis that it is now no longer possible to work something out 'on the bag of a fag packet', it examined the dreadful decisions taken at MOfP since the smoking ban was introduced by the Blair government.

The conclusion was that people use napkins now.

Key learning points for the team: Of zero interest now, people vape.

Miscellaneous Stuff

A long-held ambition of the out-going Chief Curator, this display told the stories of his time at the museum.

With a focus on the exceptionally dull elements of the collection which we could never previously bring ourselves to focus on, the Development team sort funding on many occasions and failed at all times.

Fortunately for us Covid 19 led to the closure of the museum for a 6 month period which enabled us to claim the poor performance was only because we were closed. It would have been awful anyway.

Key learning points for the team: Retirement was overdue.

Ghosted

Ghosted

A dark tale of Museum recruitment nightmares

Come and see us for an interview and never hear back again!

Competitive ticket prices

Degree or similar experience essential

Tickets Unavailable
Museum of Forward Planning

Ghosted

Museum recruitment nightmares - Originally scheduled to run to just two rooms, in the end this project grew to cover not just our museum, but countless others.

Reviewing countless horrific recruitment experiences through the eyes of the failed applicant, and telling the story entirely through screams, poorly laid out job profiles and misleading salary promises, we told the story of why people fail to get jobs that are destined for the niece of the Treasurer, and why everyone else is ghosted.

Key learning points for the team: No feedback available

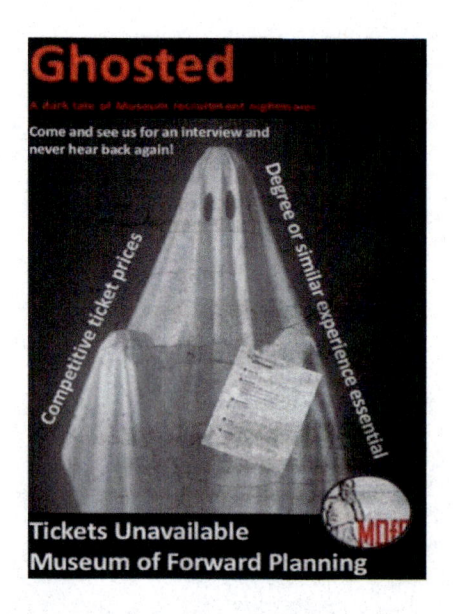

Cancellation Cake
Heathy well-being promoted through budget cuts

DON't LET THEM EAT CAKE

Staff only
Museum of Forward Planning

Don't let them eat cake

This threw open the doors and shone a light on the culture of museums and heritage organisations, where decent salaries are basically replaced with the promise of stale cake from the staff canteen.

Bringing the stories of our back of house teams to the floor, we were able to highlight the deep depression that came from our Head of Wellbeing banning cake in an effort to improve the health of our sugar-enriched teams.

The café was a hit. **Key learning points for the team: If cake is all we have. Let us keep it.**

But this doesn't scan.

Our retrospective looking back at some of the greatest howlers of our operational planning. Featuring spotlights that flickered, a tensator barrier maze that changed on an hourly basis and a range of interactive devices that failed to interact and which were made from almost exclusively unavailable parts.

A critical success, yet an operational nightmare.

No visitor numbers were recorded as the scanning systems and new ticketing system failed on the first day and IT were unable to recover the data.

Key learning points for the team: nothing at all. All these mistakes will always be repeated.

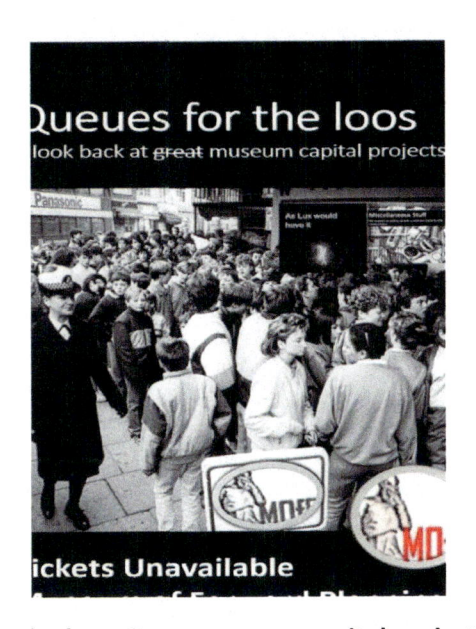

Queues for the loo - Great museum capital projects

A look back at some of the greatest white elephants of all time. Museums that were created at huge cost and won every single architectural prize that was available.

Sadly, these museums were largely impossible to operate, and this led to huge queues for both the lifts and the toilets which had been value engineered out and were, as a result, entirely insufficient.

The experience created was both breathtakingly beautiful and logistically impossible.

MUSEUM-SPLAINING

Tickets Unavailable
Museum of Forward Planning

Museum-Splaining

As we welcomed our communities to co-create and co-curate with us, we were disgusted to find that they had both an interest in the museum and a view on the community and society which we so eagerly wanted to engage with (at arms-length).

The resultant exhibition was the first time NATO had been involved in resolving a creative dispute, and involved our team of highly trained academics explaining the lives of people in the community they barely understood, without any recourse to the community itself.

Key learning points for the team: Keep the community at arm's length.

Conclusion

As can be seen. The reason all these exhibitions, and countless others, failed is Marketing.

If the Marketing had worked we would not only be successful, but real. On the odd occasion we have had a success that has been exclusively due to the brilliant content.

We will not be covering the dark arts of Media and PR, and as a Board of Trustees MOfP has chosen to largely ignore sociable media – leaving Geoff to do 'his thing, which seems to involve a stream of consciousness and quite a few GDPR and Governance concerns, being aired publicly.

But who do we market to?

Who visits us?

This brings us on to our next chapter – finding our audience.

Chapter 12

Finding 'OUR' Audience

It's fine to work hard, look after the collections we are custodians of, maximise the income from the copyright options we have available, and create endless meetings and bureaucracy. But what's the point?

Who are we doing it all for?

Every Museum Board will conclude, even though the front of house team know many of their visitors by name and can talk you through their different visiting behaviours and needs, it is necessary to pay a team of consultants to identify exactly who visits the museum and why.

At some point in the process there will be an animated discussion about those people who do not visit the museum. Where are they in all this? The answer is they are somewhere more fun than they actually want to visit. While you could spend a huge amount of money and effort seducing non-visitors to your site. They will more than likely visit, prove to themselves it was not for them anyway, and never come again. However, you'll need to do this anyway.

At the end of an extensive and expensive programme of research work with the respected agency Monte-Holstein-Mackerel we were as surprised as you are to find our visitor types were precisely the same as the visitor types Monte-Holstein-Mackerel had identified everywhere else (for a similar fee). It was a complete puzzle to be honest.

It's not enough to identify who these people are – your audiences – you then have to make sure everyone learns about them and you design everything you do to suit them*

until someone in the digital and technology teams mentions personas, then you create a new lot

Figure 45 - Visit properly - our audience segregation work

Our Audience Types

Thanks to a large cash transfer, everyone in our site is now aware of the very specific audience types MOfP attracts. For the sake of form we have included the badly formatted slides we received in exchange for our souls below

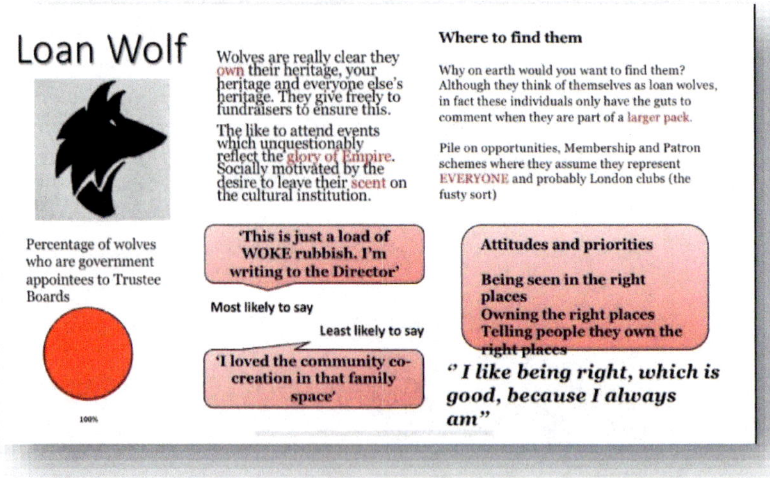

Loan Wolf

Wolves are really clear they own their heritage, your heritage and everyone else's heritage. They give freely to fundraisers to ensure this.

The like to attend events which unquestionably reflect the glory of Empire. Socially motivated by the desire to leave their scent on the cultural institution.

Percentage of wolves who are government appointees to Trustee Boards

100%

Most likely to say
'This is just a load of WOKE rubbish. I'm writing to the Director'

Least likely to say
'I loved the community co-creation in that family space'

Where to find them

Why on earth would you want to find them? Although they think of themselves as loan wolves, in fact these individuals only have the guts to comment when they are part of a larger pack.

Pile on opportunities, Membership and Patron schemes where they assume they represent EVERYONE and probably London clubs (the fusty sort)

Attitudes and priorities
- Being seen in the right places
- Owning the right places
- Telling people they own the right places

" I like being right, which is good, because I always am"

Figure 46 - Loan Wolf

Figure 47 - Lost?

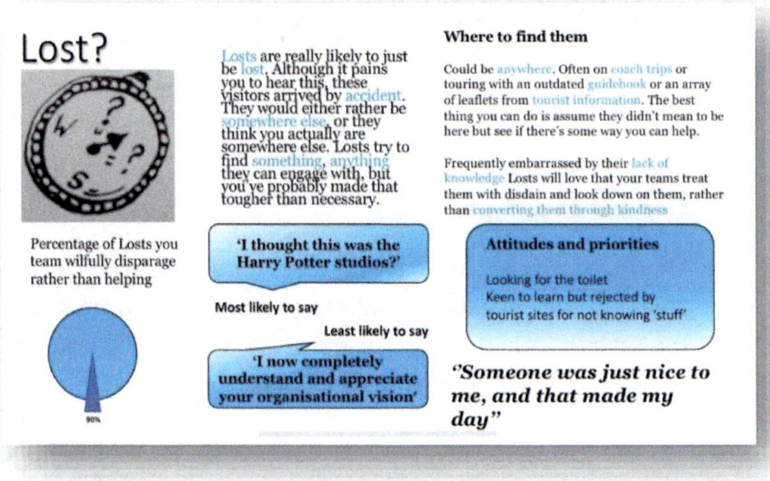

Lost?

Losts are really likely to just be lost. Although it pains you to hear this, these visitors arrived by accident. They would either rather be somewhere else, or they think you actually are somewhere else. Losts try to find something, anything they can engage with, but you've probably made that tougher than necessary.

Percentage of Losts you team wilfully disparage rather than helping

90%

Most likely to say
'I thought this was the Harry Potter studios?'

Least likely to say
'I now completely understand and appreciate your organisational vision'

Where to find them

Could be anywhere. Often on coach trips or touring with an outdated guidebook or an array of leaflets from tourist information. The best thing you can do is assume they didn't mean to be here but see if there's some way you can help.

Frequently embarrassed by their lack of knowledge Losts will love that your teams treat them with disdain and look down on them, rather than converting them through kindness

Attitudes and priorities
- Looking for the toilet
- Keen to learn but rejected by tourist sites for not knowing 'stuff'

"Someone was just nice to me, and that made my day"

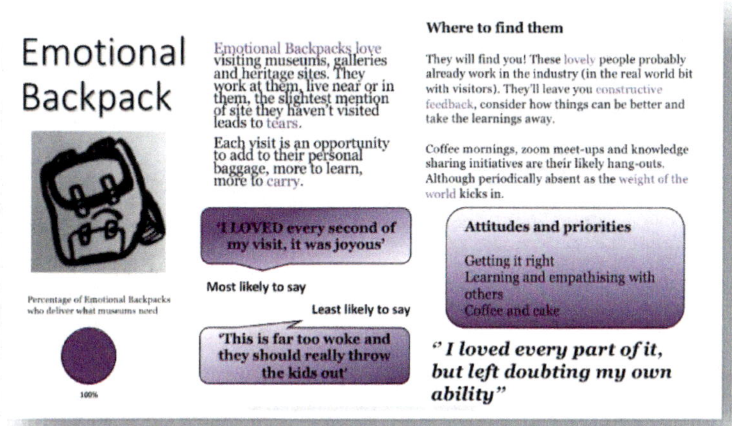

Emotional Backpack

Emotional Backpacks love visiting museums, galleries and heritage sites. They work at them, live near or in them, the slightest mention of site they haven't visited leads to tears.

Each visit is an opportunity to add to their personal baggage, more to learn, more to carry.

Where to find them

They will find you! These lovely people probably already work in the industry (in the real world bit with visitors). They'll leave you constructive feedback, consider how things can be better and take the learnings away.

Coffee mornings, zoom meet-ups and knowledge sharing initiatives are their likely hang-outs. Although periodically absent as the weight of the world kicks in.

Percentage of Emotional Backpacks who deliver what museums need: 100%

Most likely to say: 'I LOVED every second of my visit, it was joyous'

Least likely to say: 'This is far too woke and they should really throw the kids out'

Attitudes and priorities
- Getting it right
- Learning and empathising with others
- Coffee and cake

" I loved every part of it, but left doubting my own ability"

Figure 48 - Emotional Backpacker

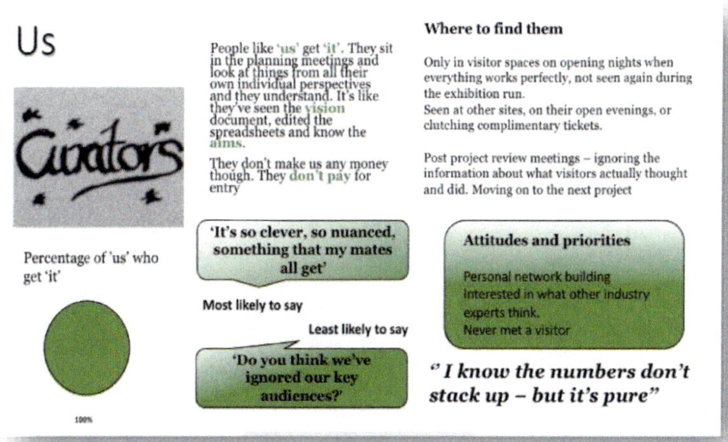

Us

People like 'us' get 'it'. They sit in the planning meetings and look at things from all their own individual perspectives and they understand. It's like they've seen the vision document, edited the spreadsheets and know the aims.

They don't make us any money though. They don't pay for entry.

Where to find them

Only in visitor spaces on opening nights when everything works perfectly, not seen again during the exhibition run.
Seen at other sites, on their open evenings, or clutching complimentary tickets.

Post project review meetings – ignoring the information about what visitors actually thought and did. Moving on to the next project

Percentage of 'us' who get 'it': 100%

Most likely to say: 'It's so clever, so nuanced, something that my mates all get'

Least likely to say: 'Do you think we've ignored our key audiences?'

Attitudes and priorities
- Personal network building
- Interested in what other industry experts think.
- Never met a visitor

" I know the numbers don't stack up – but it's pure"

Figure 49 - Us

Persecuted Pedant

Pedants. They have no interest in your site unless its' to find the numerous errors your teams will have made.

You can MAKE there day through a well-place typo, accidentally getting a date wrong or even being completely right, but not right in their book.

Percentage of interpretation panels that will contain an error despite best efforts

100%

Where to find them

Usually in the back part of the exhibition, in that area where you thought nobody would go, reading that interpretation panel you are least happy with, but, well budgets, timescales, issues with the exhibition supplier, problems with the loan agreements.

Same place two days later – seeing if you fixed the issue or if you DON'T CARE.

'I think you'll find it sank on it's maiden voyage'

Most likely to say

Least likely to say

'Oh, I apologise, you clearly are right'

Attitudes and priorities

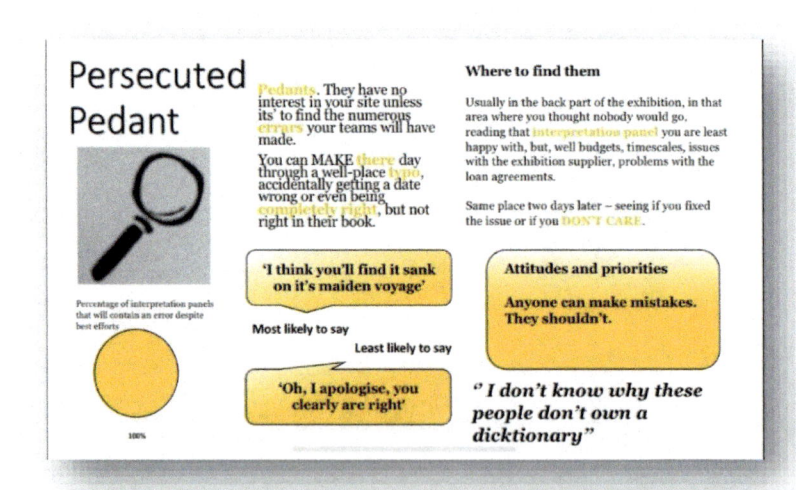

Anyone can make mistakes. They shouldn't.

" I don't know why these people don't own a dicktionary"

Figure 50 - Persecuted pedant

Somnambulant Scowler

Somnambulant Scowlers make up a huge portion of your visitor numbers but you like to pretend they don't. Accompanying friends or meeting family, they are bored before they arrive and you never do enough to engage them because – why would you dumb down?

Percentage of learning points retained after visit

100%

Where to find them

You know that scruffy 'rest and recuperation' area that the curators are always trying to do away with so they can fill it with more collection? They're there. Whole gangs of them.

A few small changes could drag these individuals into the waking daydream that's your cultural site. It might feel like dumbing down, but it's **actually engaging** people in what you do!

'I really enjoyed the café. Good to have a break'

Most likely to say

Least likely to say

'I recall a number of key learning outcomes that enriched my day'

Attitudes and priorities

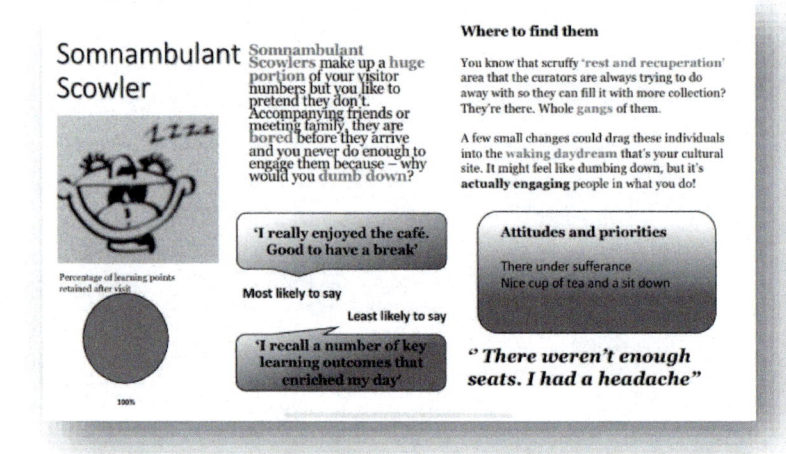

There under sufferance
Nice cup of tea and a sit down

" There weren't enough seats. I had a headache"

Figure 51 - Somnambulant scowler

So, what does this mean for us at MOfP?

Our audience breaks down by percentage as follows.

Type	Percentage
Loan Wolf	3%
Lost?	25%
Emotional Backpacker	12%
Us	50%
Persecuted Pedant	8%
Somnambulant Scowler	2%

Our Board have identified the priority audience types as:

- Somnambulant Scowlers
- Loan Wolves

We've been working to this audience segregation model for 10 years now and the plan has delivered no measurable improvement.

Measuring Success

Fortunately, we know how to measure whether we have been successful. On every occasion we run an exhibition we ask our consultants to come and measure the performance.

The process is simple, the agency identifies who our key audiences are. They then interview random visitors and are able to use the sample to factor up the feedback and create an incredibly accurate picture of the audience who attended.

In recent years individual exhibitions have been graded with a net promoter score of at least 97% and we have almost precisely matched the predicted audience segregation model the agency predicted. They are that good!

But what about those that don't visit?

I mean. Who cares? They're happier in the theme park down the road anyway.

Personas

In the past we only needed to be mis-sold an audience segregation model. But times change and it is now necessary for all museums to consider the different personas who will be using and accessing your museum both onsite, and online. Some of these people are the same, but we like to keep a degree of separation and pay for the work to be done twice.

At MOfP we have a complex persona model but don't let that put you off considering persona types yourself – you can start with something much more basic than we have.

Figure 52 is our current persona model, and everything we do is looked at through both the lens of the audience segregations, and the personas themselves.

Having completed this detailed work, we then junk it all and go with the gut instinct of the Board, or as we call it 'Chaos

Theory'.

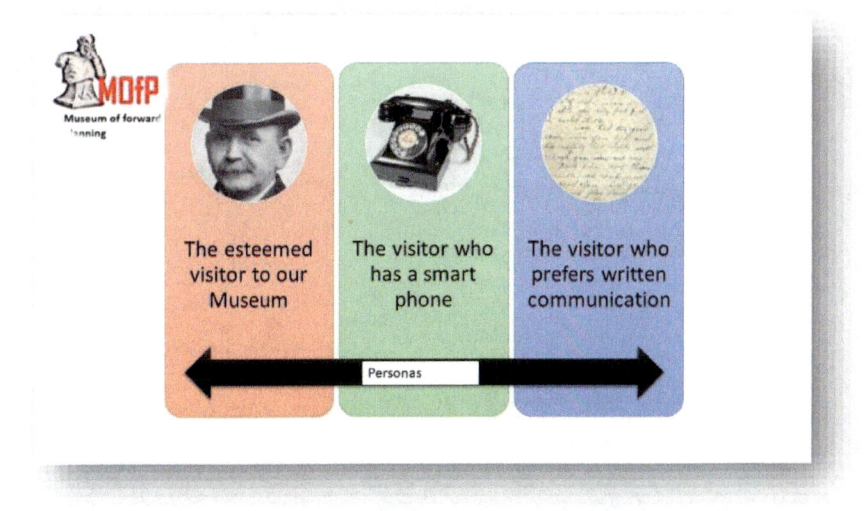

Figure 52 - Personas... yawn

As you can see in figure 51 our up-to-the-minute research has identified three main personas

- The esteemed visitor to our museum (who respect and value)
- The visitor who has a smart phone (who we revile)
- The visitor who prefers to write letters to us (who we ignore)

We don't need to consider personas any further. Nobody will.

A brief announcement about our association with Cads in Museums

Press Update

Cads in Museums

The team at MOfP are unexpectedly happy to be able to announce the Board's decision to signal a new partnership with **Cads in Museums**

In the coming months we will be adopting the key planks of the Cads In Museums Manifesto as we seek to secure future funding streams.

- Our Board recruitment will focus exclusively on former Tory MP's* and old Etonians
- Our Development team will seeks funding from questionable sources and soon to be disgraced business models
- We will defend our right to **retain** all looted elements of our collection, without an effort to **explain** our stance
- On the annual Cad's Takeover Day the Board will upend management policies and best practice and instead adopt the approaches recommended in the Daily Express
- Tofu, Veganuary and generally Wokery will be purged

*we expect to be spoilt for choice soon

Quotes for journalists
'This is a fantastic opportunity for us to embrace the kind of approach which should ensure funding for our new outpost in Grantham'
Chair of the Trustees

'FFS, I just can't even...'
Outgoing Head of Media and PR

'Don't use the Terry Thomas image, they'll all think smoking is okay again and it isn't'
Beleaguered Head of Visitor Experience

Cads In Museums

Part 4

It's all about money

Chapter 13

All about the money – Income Streaming

Are you a Member?

Can we be honest? Our relationship with our members is the very definition of 'complicated'.

We need our Members, they are a brilliant source of income, a core group of passionate supporters, hugely engaged and interested, and the people we know are most like 'us' (see previous Audiences work).

But we also hate our members. They complain constantly. They dislike change. They believe they own our museum, our collections, and our staff. They don't ever want to queue. They want special places, special memories, and special treatment. We want their money.

We shouldn't be honest, should we?

MOfP Members

Our Membership scheme is absolutely unique. We use it as a way to raise money and insult our supporters at the same time.

We prize the fact our Members continue to demand the best from us at the lowest possible price and regardless of anything that makes life harder for us. Pandemics, fire, floods, we know Members will still come and will still want a discount coffee.

Our most successful recruitment drive nailed what we expect from our Members.

M.O.R.O.N
Members Opposing Reality Or Normality

WE NEED YOU!

Tickets Unavailable
Museum of Forward Planning

Figure 53 - MORON poster

M.O.R.O.N

What was the unique idea?

We wanted to recognise many of the demands of our Membership are moronic. Members simultaneously want everything to be free or as cheap as possible, want special treatment every time and want to have things exactly as they have always been – whilst simultaneously complaining each time we try to do something new because they hate change.

Don't even change the sandwiches. But do make them interesting in a standard way, and ensure they are priced as they were in 1980 when the Membership was first sold.

Sign up number from campaign 109,000

Number of Members we had to ban 108,999

Figure 54 - Pratrons

PRATRONS

What even is a Patron?

We are aware that it's hard to know what the difference is between a Patron and a member. Thankfully we have a clear hierarchy. Patrons pay much more for the same benefits, and we write their names on different walls of the museum at different times.

(We have learned that we need to make sure any names on walls can be easily removed, this ensures we are future-proofed against the time when the Patron is disgraced for something which we can all say we suspected was always the case – once the Netflix documentary series hits our screens.

Legacies

Feeling a bit sick?

The need to gain funding through new channels has left many museums struggling to find options that can work for them.

With an ageing demographic visiting our museum as our outdated displays deliver reducing returns, we now need to think about what happens when this audience is gone.

When they're gone, we hope to simultaneously get rich quickly, and to have to deal with far fewer visitors. There is no way this can be bad!

If your museum isn't already targeting legacies and bequests, what are you doing? How are you even paying for benches?!

Make only donations Leave only legacies

Figure 55 - The importance of leaving a legacy

Our recent campaign offered anyone leaving us a legacy a free Parker Pen or Marks and Spencer vouchers to the value of £20 and was an absolute hit.

We also like to focus on our volunteers – not only are they a key stakeholder group of a certain age, but they are passionate about the museum. In addition, we can control the temperature on our site, so in the winter... well... they may get a little cold.

Chapter 14

Selling out

Retail excellence in museums is something we should all strive to achieve. Here at MOfP it's often a challenge to achieve this alongside the core work of our organisation (keeping the Trustees happy).

In order to achieve any kind of balance we realised the best approach is to produce everything we create both as a product, and as a postcard. This means that Trustee who is always banging on about postcards is now finally happy, and when the oil runs out we will be able to heat the museum using fire fuelled entirely by excess postcards.

Figure 56 - Sodding postcards

The corkboard above neatly illustrates some of our worst sellers.

1. *How we see museums – an institutional study*
2. *Postcard depicting the ever popular 'I prefer their earlier stuff' slogan*
3. *Our industry leading 'Circle of career fire'.*
4. *Queue here – like nobody's watching.*

How do we choose our range?

Thanks to the brave new world of dropshipping (we had to look it up too), we no longer need to worry about choosing a bespoke product range that reflects our sites and our proposition. Instead we simply joined up to a warehousing organisation situated in a high skill, low wage economy – to be fair that's now the UK – and they paste our logo onto any old tat.

Of course, we still ensure that for every exhibition our curators produce a detailed and extensive catalogue. Covid impacts meant that as we saw reduced visitor numbers and operated on tighter budgets we've been able to use the remainder stock to build a storehouse for the other remainder stock we continue to build.

Personality matters

Don't be afraid to reflect the personality of your museum in the products you sell. In our case we trade on our cynicism and the chip on the shoulder of all front of house staff in the sector.

Best sellers include our 'nobody has suffered like the curators' mug (which we are proud to share was a phrase actually uttered during a wash-up meeting). Yes, we were baffled too.

Figure 57 - Mugs

It is important to reflect the many voices of your teams though.

Not least retail colleagues. They'll happily set up an area in your giftshop for the 'we told you this was shit and wouldn't sell' collection which the senior team have foisted upon them.

Sales

At times you will need to do something to shift the excess stock which is threatening to swamp the organisation. We have trialled a number of methods to deliver this.

Our 'Car Boot Sale' has been hugely successful. Not only did it allow us to clear a lot of old product that nobody wanted to purchase, we also acquired an early version of the kids game 'Operation' that looks like it might work if we can find the right batteries. We were also able to ship out quite a large quantity of the museum collection which we should probably have deaccessioned first, but has nonetheless enabled us to provide more storage for the latest donations and acquisitions.

Monetising the collection

This can be a thorny issue.

Many people believe that monetising the collection without careful thought can be crass and undermines the great work we do to make sure our visitors understand they are really not worthy to see, let alone touch, the items that we hold for the good of the Nation.

This seems a little over the top.

We've been able to produce replicas of many items in our collection, some as good as the originals (which now adorn the walls of some of our less ethical supporters!).

MOfP also pioneers best practice in bringing together the commercial and charitable strands of our work. The recent

'Urn as you go' exhibition featured a range of reconditioned amusement arcade 'grab-games' which have proved incredibly popular with young and old alike. These have enabled us to reduce the size of our collection store and increase our retail income at the same time. Effectively we have been able to sell tickets for our shop!

Figure 58 - Pay as you urn - an example of exciting innovation

Chapter 15

Catering

Any visit to a museum is essentially about visiting the café.

Yes the displays can be mildly interesting, perhaps the family activity can be an opportunity to bond over the pots of glue and the crepe paper, but other than the toilets, the café is the only place visitors are sure to dwell in.

If increasing dwell time is something your Senior Leadership Team are focussed on, then a simple solution is incredibly slow service in the museum café.

What are the aims of your café?

Too few museums truly consider the aims of the café they manage.

The main aim is clearly to take as much money from visitors as possible, whilst offering very little food. At MOfP we have also considered the audiences who visit. We haven't used the persona or audience segregation models which are mentioned elsewhere – that would be crazy talk – Instead we have created an entirely different approach.

Many museum visitors using the café are families. They'll naturally be short of money in these straightened times and will often take the approach of buying one or two items to share between them in an attempt to reduce the headline cost. To counter this, we only make our food and drink purchases available in MASSIVE portions. This means that while a family might be relatively well fed on one piece of cake – they'll still damn well pay £13.99 for the slice.

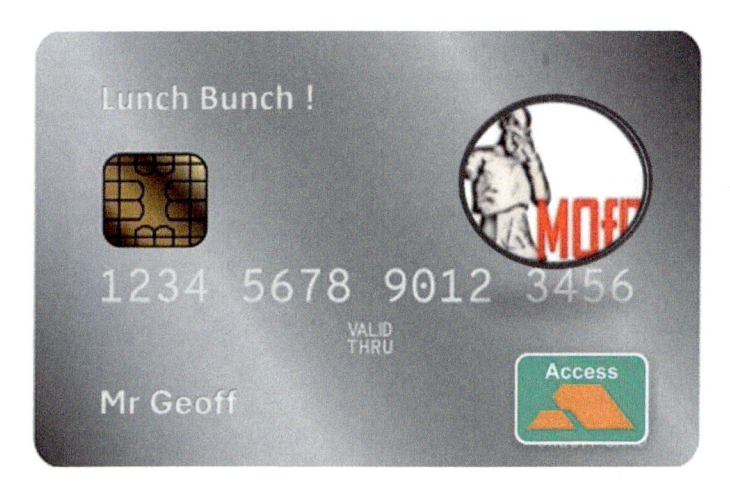

Figure 59 - Cake is no longer beyond the reach of mortals and museum staff

As you can see from figure 58 we are happy to innovate to ensure we remain affordable. Our 'Lunch Bunch' credit card allows visitors to spread the cost of a piece of cake over a number of years, at a relatively low rate of interest.

Seasonal Offers

Seasonal offers are also a MUST, if you can't produce a pumpkin flavoured milkshake in October, why do you even bother?

Amongst our recent success stories, #FLANUARY saw us offer discounted flans to visitors and led to a definite increase in optimism for our commercial director, which we hope one day to translate into actual sales.

Figure 60 - Flantastic! Another great promotion

Chapter 16

Capital project punishment.
How to deal with the white elephant

It's finally happened. Your museum has basically won the lottery.

After an intensive round of fundraising, many months filling out grant applications, and the sacrificing of all you stood for in terms of ethics and values, your museum is now going to build that amazing capital project your Board have been dreaming of since the late 1920's.

Will it be everything you wished for?

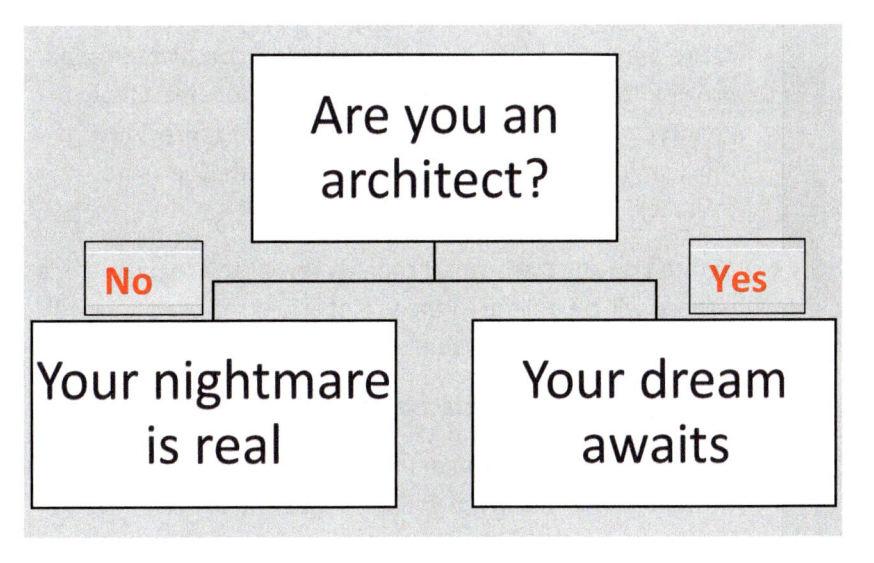

Figure 61 - Architectural outcomes

Award winning

From the start you know that the museum capital project you are involved in will be award winning.

The people who judge and present the awards will be almost exclusively designers and architects. So that's great. It's lovely to be appreciated by your peers. However, these people are not your peers if you are a museum. These people are architects. They only attend museum openings and the closure periods when museums are being remodelled so that the internal plumbing, glass panelling and flat roof can be revisited in order to repair the damage done to visitors and your collection by the building created to house them.

What are the issues going to be?

There are going to be issues with the final completed capital project. Despite the fact you are going to appoint a team of architects that have famously won awards for previous museum projects, they are going to replicate the same mistakes.

Before you start let's run through a few of the regular issues – these will be built in to the project from the start – we can get on to what will be value engineered out later.

Mistakes that will be designed in

It is worth running through the errors that will be built in from the start and which you consequently will not have to worry about.

In advance of taking over the new building, it will be worth popping to another museum that is a few years ahead of you in the process so you can discuss coping mechanisms with their maintenance and finance teams and begin work on the grant application to rectify the issues.

Area of focus	Built in issue
	Fittings and fixtures Be-spoke and beautifully designed the building will be resplendent with hand-made, artisan created fittings. Once the building is a year old these will all be impossible to source. You'll have to get your lightbulbs from Poundland.
	Access Despite the long-standing accessibility requirements which are actually enshrined in law, large parts of your *brand-new, purpose-built* museum will be totally inaccessible. This will be a complete surprise to everyone.
	It's cold inside. The main doors will be stuck open, the internal doors will be too heavy The BMS system will not have been designed to take into account that anyone may pass in and our of the spaces that have been created for people to pass in and out of. You'll buy curtains.

	Budget You will blow the budget, including the contingency, which the designer assumed was really petty cash. You will still not have enough money to complete the project, and this is where you get into the serious elements of value engineering
	Connectivity Wi-Fi, connectivity for IT, power. All key in the modern age. Yet, your new museum will be the most effective Faraday cage that has ever been created. The power points will not be anywhere you need them, and the data points will always be the wrong category.

Where's the value?

There are some vital areas of any design that can be removed with a minimal impact on the staff that matter.

- **Changing rooms** – these are always over-specified. It's quite possible for your front of house staff (the only ones that actually need to wear a uniform) to get changed in the nearby bus stop. That's why all Project Managers remove any reasonable changing space as an easy way to increase gallery floorspace. The Executive team have never considered staff need to change into their uniforms. This is despite the fact the staff handbook specifies that staff MUST NOT wear their uniforms outside work. Still, cut these spaces first.

- **Toilets** – when you look on the plans there will be toilets everywhere. Who even uses the toilet in a museum apart from all the visitors who come, anyone who has kids, large parts of the ageing demographic you rely on? The toilets can definitely be cut in huge numbers. There's never a queue on the swanky opening nights when there are only 100 people present in a museum that was actually designed to take 20,000 visitors a day.

- **Lifts**- These seem very expensive! Why would we need lifts that are reliable and efficient? It's not as if we use them for transporting thousands of visitors a year around the site, moving the collection from space to space, or even just for getting staff to their posts quickly.

LIFTS OFF – An illustration of the issue

Projected visitor numbers

Projected lift users

Projected stair users.

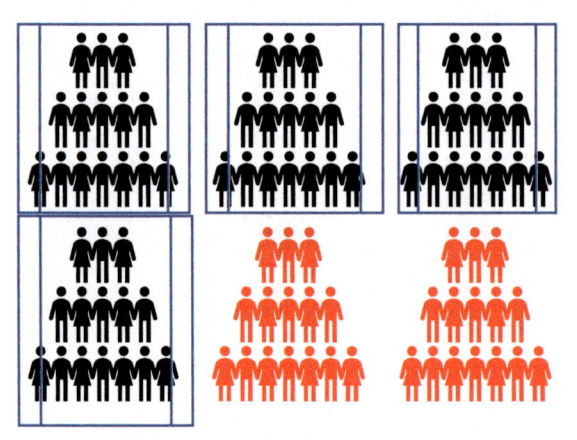

Number of lifts required (4)

Projected visitor numbers

Value engineered lifts(2)   Projected stair users.

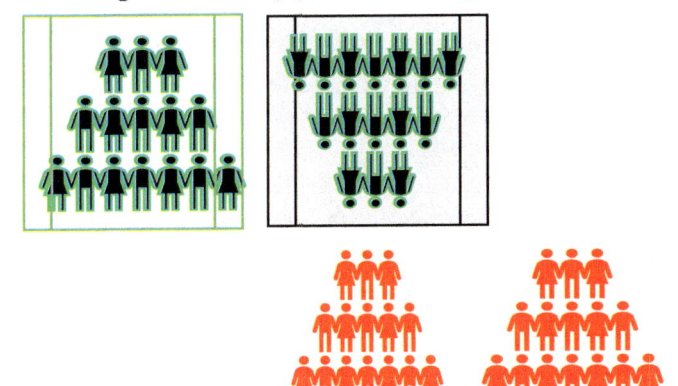

Where did half the lift users go?

A large number of visitors will never, ever see anything beyond your principle floor, because life is short. They left.

In addition, pay very careful attention to the music you play in the lifts. If the architects have not only reduced the number but reduced the quality, the one investment you should make is in a good sound system. Visitors will be spending a lot of time in there after all!

The grand vision

What matters most is the vision, and ensuring that reality does not taint that vision.

For this reason, it is essential that we keep the operational, maintenance and finance teams as far away as possible from the planning and development stages.

Only once the planning permission is in, the deal sealed and the walls are up, should you admit any members of the operational teams. This is best set up as an exciting 'hard hat' tour, where the team can be whizzed around the new real estate, without being given time to consider the elements that they know are missing.

Any questions can be met with the simple comment 'the architects are award winning' and that will be sufficient to close down that conversation.

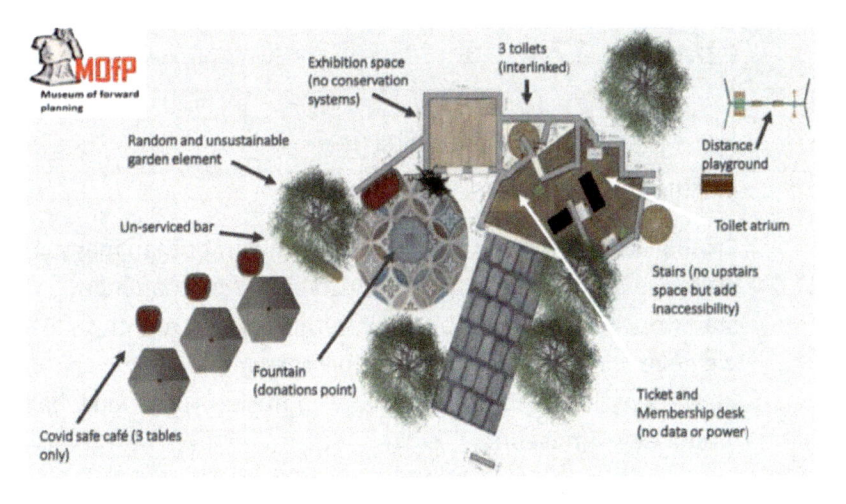

Figure 62 - One of many failed designs for future museums

Conclusion

The work on a new building and delivering a capital project is never done. As it completed the project team will move on to deliver a new and exciting re-imagining of a museum or gallery, which will look a lot like yours but with more expensive light fittings that are easier to source.

You meanwhile, will be left to begin work on the corrective projects which will aim to fix the roof, provide Wi-Fi and install portacabins that can be used to create changing spaces and toilets for the staff who we all value incredibly highly (although who will have seen their numbers cut so that we can pay the bills outstanding for the capital project overspend – in hindsight perhaps that is why the architects felt we needed fewer changing rooms?

Chapter 17

Re-re-imaging the future
Closing thoughts

Closing is always tricky. It happens much earlier than many visitors expect, and it happens much less often than many staff hope. But we must bring everything we do to a close. If we never closed down a thought process we would never deliver anything without chaos and confusion, and then what would be? A museum.

The team at MOfP love museums, they work in one and although it isn't real, it feels like an organisation that might just exist in different parts of the real world. It feels like somewhere that could exist at that point where the real world impinges on the thoughts and dreams of a bunch of people who just want visitors to have a good time, see exciting things and learn stuff.

This brief guide can only touch, imperfectly, on the challenges and joys that are integral to the operation of a museum and central to the ongoing stress of those who work within it.

It's our sincere hope that by laughing at the many repeated patterns we have identified here, we can all acknowledge that sometimes the way the sector works is completely absurd, and to recognise that is both absolutely fine (normal when humans are involved), but also something we should actually deal with too.

In the meantime, we all just need to keep on re-re-imagining, immerse ourselves in an interactive future, and look for more ways to do more, with less, more often, with greater enthusiasm and rising levels of efficiency.

Acknowledgements

The Museum of Forward Planning (MOfP) began as a fever dream during the Covid lockdowns of 2019-20. It was obvious that, as museums and galleries attempted to re-open, we were dealing with a range of truly first-world problems, which were still vital for us to solve.

When we did re-open, visitors often cried (in a good way) that they could see the collections and staff they loved.

I genuinely love working in museums. I love the openness, the fact that everyone works together, the way in which we all share. During Covid that was more apparent than ever.

So it's only right to acknowledge so many friends who have shared their mad stories about museum life, the many people who have unintentionally said something that ended up as a post on the account, and the people that discouraged me from doing this at all.

Without the Head of PR who threatened me with death if I ever ran a fake twitter account about the real world.

Without the organisers and followers of MuseumsShowoff.

Without the countless brilliant and funny people.

And without almost everyone at the V&A who thinks I work there because it sounds just like their life... but I don't so it isn't.. even if it is.

There wouldn't be this daft little book.

Hope you laughed and only cringed on occasion

Access, 96, 144
architects, 90, 143, 149, 150
Audience, 119, 120
barriers, 42, 53, 86, 87, 88, 99
Barriers, 86
Budget, 145
budgets, 33, 53, 84, 89
cake, 114, 140
capacity, 35, 93
career, 23, 29, 31, 32, 33, 39, 47, 49, 56, 75, 104
Career, 29
Careering off, 56
Catering, 8, 27, 139
Changing rooms, 145
collection, 16, 25, 26, 63, 67, 80, 94, 100, 101, 103, 104, 108, 112, 136, 137, 138, 143, 146
Collection, 100, 103, 108
Collections, 24, 25, 62, 63, 101, 104
Collections Care, 24, 25
Communication approaches. *See*
Competence, 38
Competencies, 39
Connectivity, 145
Curatorial, 24, 59, 87
Customer Service, 70, 72

Doing more, with less, more often, 49
elephant, 90
exhibition, 13, 25, 26, 34, 51, 57, 58, 59, 65, 69, 71, 73, 78, 86, 91, 92, 93, 94, 95, 96, 97, 98, 108, 109, 111, 117, 124
Exhibition, 92, 95
Feedback, 97
Fittings and fixtures, 144
FOH, 93
Front of House, 26, 43
Full Collins, 105
immerse, 152
interpretation, 16, 35, 62, 110
Inventory, 71, 104
Legacies, 132
Lifts, 146
Management, 26, 36, 37, 44
Marketing, 98, 107, 118
Maximum shame, *52*
Measuring, 124
meetings, 21, 68, 89, 95, 119
Member, 129
Messy Matrix Structure, *14*
Motivation, 41
Multi-organisational ghosting, 55

Museum-Splaining, 117
Myth, 84
Operating, 61
Operations, 62, 64, 66, 67, 68, 70, 71, 88
organisational, 13
Patron, 132
Personal Development, 36
Personas, 125
Postcard, 135
programme, 34, 35, 36, 45, 46, 51, 57, 58, 66, 119
Recruitment, 75
Re-re-imaging, 151
Re-re-imagining, 10
Resilience, 47
Retail, 24, 27, 134
Sales, 137
Senior Leadership Team, 19, 20
signage, 79, 81, 86, 99
Signage, 25, 79, 81
Smile Like You Mean It, 73, 74
Staff Survey, 44
Staffing, 89, 94

Strategy, 49, 50
SWOT, 24, 25, 26
The clarity of ignorance, 54
The Executive Team, 17
The Knowable, 54
The Visitor Journey, 76
toilets, 12, 32, 35, 63, 78, 116, 139, 146, 150
Toilets, 146
Triple 'T' Test, *64*
Trustees, 15, 16, 20, 26, 38, 47, 57, 58, 61, 101, 118
vision, 10, 11, 38, 39, 100, 149
visitor, 11, 15, 35, 54, 58, 61, 63, 64, 67, 69, 70, 71, 74, 76, 77, 78, 80, 86, 90, 96, 99, 101, 107, 108, 115, 119, 126, 135, 147, 148
Visitor, 35, 58, 64, 74, 76, 78, 87, 96, 97
Visitors, 24, 25, 61, 62, 63, 81, 94, 109
Wellbeing, 41, 114
Workload, 89

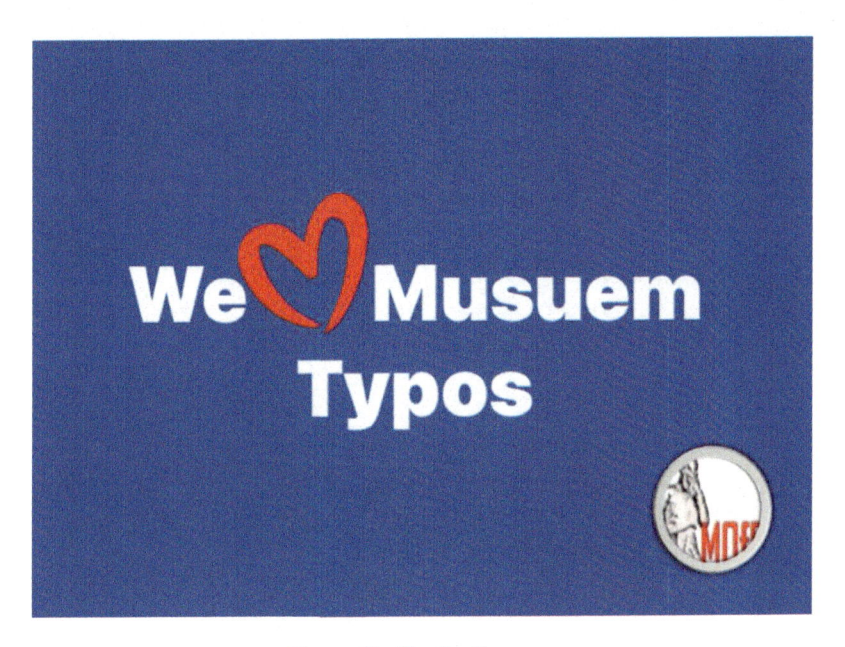

Figure 63 - The Truth

Printed in Great Britain
by Amazon